NEWMAN AND GADAMER

AAR

American Academy of Religion
Reflection and Theory in the Study of Religion

Editor
David E. Klemm

Number 10
NEWMAN AND GADAMER
Toward a Hermeneutics of Religious Knowledge

by
Thomas K. Carr

NEWMAN AND GADAMER
Toward a Hermeneutics of Religious Knowledge

by
Thomas K. Carr

Scholars Press
Atlanta, Georgia

NEWMAN AND GADAMER
Toward a Hermeneutics of Religious Knowledge

by
Thomas K. Carr

© 1996
The American Academy of Religion

Library of Congress Cataloging in Publication Data

Carr, Thomas K., 1962–
    Newman and Gadamer : toward a hermeneutics of religious knowledge
/ by Thomas K. Carr.
        p.   cm. — (AAR reflection and theory in the study of religion ;
no. 10)
    Includes bibliographical references.
    ISBN 0-7885-0303-0 (cloth : alk. paper). — ISBN 0-7885-0304-9
(paper : alk. paper)
    1. Newman, John Henry, 1801–1890.   2. Gadamer, Hans Georg, 1900–   .
I. Title.   II. Series.
BX4705.N5C29 1996
282'.092—dc20
                                                                96-28988
                                                                CIP

Printed in the United States of America
on acid-free paper

In memoriam

Laura Anne Kinsell Carr [1935-1992]

ACKNOWLEDGEMENTS

I am indeed but one in a cast of several who played a part in this project, and thus deserve my gratitude. I wish to thank Keith Ward, Regius Professor of Divinity at Oxford, who supervised the thesis that forms the basis of this book. It is his way, thankfully, to be encouraging and uplifting even when issuing sharp criticism. Thanks also go to John Macquarrie, Ian Ker, Graham Ward, Nigel Biggar, Jamie Ferreira, Jean Greisch, Ernest Nicholson, Hans-Peter Martensen, Friederike Martensen, Thorsten Fröhling, Karlfried Fröhlich, Charles Ryerson and Jean-Lup Seban, each of whom either read or discussed with me portions of my work. The Provost and administrative staff of Oriel College deserve praise for allowing me leave from my post as Junior Dean on several occasions to pursue research abroad. I wish also to acknowledge the library staff of the following institutions: the Bodleian, Oriel College, King's College London, Hamburg University, Heidelberg University, Georgetown University, the University of Virginia, George Mason University, and George Washington University. Stephen Meadows of Oriel College also deserves credit for his timely software advice. Lastly, but with the greatest passion, I wish to express a deep indebtedness to my students. Their curiosity, questions and sharp insights always sent me deeper into myself, and thus deeper into my work. Their intelligence and maturity turned our tutorials into mutually edifying dialogues instead of stiltifying duties. I consider each one a conversation partner on the way to truth.

This essay is dedicated to my wife, Andrea, our soon-to-be-born child, and to the ongoing memory of my mother, Laura Anne Kinsell Carr.

CONTENTS

PREVIEW:

In Search of a Bridge

> *Seen from the right height everything comes together:*
> *the thoughts of the philosopher,*
> *the work of the artist,*
> *and good deeds.*

> Nietzsche, *Notebooks*

In this present study I want to consider the religious epistemology of John Henry Newman (1801-1890) from an angle that will be difficult to explain. This should not be surprising to anyone familiar with the Newman industry, for the immense body of writings he left behind has in recent years lent itself to a wide variety of interpretations. Generally in Newman studies there occurs a division of labour between students of his philosophy and theology on the one hand,[1] and students of his literary art, poetry, and rhetoric on the other.[2] Though the divide is not as distinct as I make it out to be, the proponents of either side often sharing in a common pool of Newman

---

[1] John Hick, Antony Kenny, Basil Mitchell, Josef Gruber, A J Boekraad, Bernard Lonergan, Stanley Jaki (philosophy); and Martin D'Arcy, J H Walgrave, Louis Bouyer, T J Norris, David Pailin, Nicholas Lash, Owen Chadwick, Avery Dulles (theology).

[2] John Coulson, W E Houghton, D J DeLaura, Lewis Gates, Walter Jost, A N Wilson, John Holloway and George Levine.

insights, each seems to think, and no doubt with good reason, that to mix approaches is to risk diminishing the cogency of their respective arguments. But even among these two groups there are further divisions, each offering an interpretation quite at odds with the rest. To some Newman is the great defender of Roman Catholic orthodoxy, to others the harbinger of modernism;[3] some read him as an activist, others a hermit.[4] There appears therefore to be as many Newmans as there are students of his work. This equivocation is not without foundation, of course. "To live is to change" runs Newman's famous dictum, and few have ever had as a great a talent for either living or changing. Robert Pattison considers Newman "a man whose career was a succession of reversals", and concludes that such ambiguity leaves him with "impeccable credentials as a failure".[5]

Newman's career and credentials are beyond my concern here. My aim, rather, is to find a way to bridge the more foundational bifurcation in Newman studies, to unite what Newman would call "the whole man".[6] What has been lacking up to now in the study of Newman's works is a "view", to use Newman's own term of choice, from which to judge the complex whole of his thought; a view solid enough to support a consistent interpretation yet flexible enough to accommodate the vast array of Newman's changing opinions. It is difficult to say up front what such a view might entail. But

[3] Stanley Jaki considers Newman "consumed with a burning loyalty for the person sitting in the chair of Peter"; from "Newman's Assent to Reality", *Newman Today*, ed. Stanley Jaki (San Francisco: Ignatius Press, 1989), p. 219, n. 87. To which one must compare *Internationale Cardinal Newman Studien* (Sigmaringendorf: Glock u. Lutz, 1990), vol. 14 which takes up the theme of Newman and Modernism. See especially articles by J Coulson, pp. 74-84; A H Jenkins, pp. 85-94; and J H Walgrave, pp. 142-56.

[4] Compare the activist portrait of Geoffrey Faber's, *Oxford Apostles: A Character Study of the Oxford Movement* (New York: Charles Scribner's Sons, 1934), pp. 185f., with Dr. Zeno's quietist portrayal in, *John Henry Newman: His Inner Life* (San Francisco: Ignatius Press, 1987), ch. 12.

[5] Robert Pattison, *The Great Dissent: John Henry Newman and the Liberal Heresy* (New York: Oxford university Press, 1991), preface xii.

[6] Newman, *AVS*, p. 286.

Newmanian theory in general, as Walter Jost rightly points out, calls for "comprehending an object from a particular angle, in all of its relevant *practical* aspects"[7]—i.e. not from the heights of abstract theory, but within and from the existential level of words and acts, texts and interpretations. In the present case, this translates into a concern with *what* Newman thought when he thought about the act of knowing, in light of *how* he went about expressing his thought, i.e. his characteristic way of conceptualizing both the problems associated with human knowing and their solutions.

But epistemology is a big topic and this is a short book. Hence I will restrict my attention to Newman's theory of religious knowledge and its development. The central tenet of the "view" offered here is that Newman's theory of religious knowledge is best appraised, and most effectively appropriated, in light of an appeal to a philosophical discipline not normally affiliated with epistemology: aesthetics. It is my opinion, generated principally from a study of Newman's main theoretical works, and to the defence of which this book will aim, that whatever topic he undertook to examine—the development of dogma, the function of poetry, the nature of inference and assent, the ideal of a liberal education—Newman routinely operates with aesthetic principles and methods of inquiry, argumentation and judgment, however tacitly they may have been held. I want further to suggest by implication—the limited scope of my aim prohibits a detailed account—that from the perspective of this "view" it is as true to say that Newman the consummate literary stylist wrote as a theologian and philosopher as it is to say that Newman the theologian and philosopher wrote aesthetically. But more on this in a moment.

---

[7] Walter Jost, *Rhetorical Thought in John Henry Newman* (Columbia, SC: University of South Carolina Press, 1989), preface x. Italics added.

SUGGESTING A BRIDGE

The connection between Newman's epistemology and philosophical aesthetics has never been pursued at any length. This is not without good reason. Recent scholarly opinion about aesthetics has tended to relegate it as a discipline into the realms of the irrational and meaningless. Literary critic George Steiner suggests that this attitude is in part responsible for a decidedly devastating trend in scholarly discourse, especially among the humanities; a trend that disparages the aesthetic in favour of the scientific:

> There has taken place in history, economics and what are called, significantly, the 'social sciences', what one might term a fallacy of imitative form. In each of these fields, the mode of discourse still relies almost completely on word-language. But historians, economists and social scientists have tried to graft on to the verbal matrix some of the proceedings of mathematical or total rigour. Many have grown defensive about the essential provisional and aesthetic character of their own pursuits...The ambitions of scientific rigour and prophecy have seduced much historical writing from its veritable nature, which is art.[8]

This protest against what has come to be known, in Andrew Louth's words, as the "marginalisation of the aesthetic"[9] registers a development in theories of rationality that had its origins in Enlightenment models of objectivity. Following on Descartes, objective human knowledge was thought possible if, and only if, it was governed by adherence to universal laws of reason and modelled on the clearness and distinctness of mathematical logic. Eventually

---

[8] George Steiner, *Language and Silence* (London: Harmondsworth, 1969), pp. 37-38. A similar complaint can be heard in the 1980 valedictory address of Oxford's Regius Professor of History, Hugh Trevor-Roper, when he protests against the attempt to reduce history to an objective science and defends its position as "one of the arts". "The heart of a subject", says Trevor-Roper, "is not in the method but in the motor, not in the technique but in the historian". Cited in *The Times Literary Supplement*, 25 July, 1980, p. 833.

[9] Andrew Louth, *Discerning the Mystery* (Oxford: Clarendon Press, 1983), p. 10.

this assumption crept into philosophies of art. "Aesthetic rationalism" is that ideal of French neoclassicism, begun with Rousseau, that art should be produced by adhering to rigorous rules of colour, symmetry, form, etc.; and its corollary that questions of taste and aesthetic judgment are best determined by reasoned proof and argument.

Were this still the case, then the kind of rationality associated with aesthetics would have little to do with the cognitive processes involved in religious knowledge that, as described by Newman, virtually defy codification of any kind. As he writes in the *Grammar of Assent*, in matters of religion "we reason without effort and intention, or any necessary consciousness of the path that the mind takes in passing from antecedent to conclusion".[10] Yet in the person of Kant, a "newer aesthetics" was established to rival the French tradition. In his 1790 *Critique of Judgment*, Kant writes of artistic genius that in its free play and autonomy it is able to escape the sort of legislation normally associated with other forms of reason. The artist is one whose standard of beauty is within. According to Kant, the rule by which art is judged emerges not through methodological calculation but through *ingenium*, the genius of inspired understanding. "In our general estimate of beauty", he writes, "we seek its standard *a priori* in ourselves, and, that the aesthetic faculty is itself legislative in respect of the judgment whether anything is beautiful or not".[11] This indeed brings us closer to Newman's analysis of the more intuitive side of religious knowledge and, as we shall see, to his own theory of inspired subjectivity.

But as I will explain below, Kant's theory has its own set of problems. For one thing, in arguing for autonomy, Kant effectively divorces aesthetic judgment from communal taste and criticism, leaving aesthetics squarely within the realm of subjectivity. And if Newman wants to have said anything about religious knowledge, it is

[10] Newman, *GA*, p. 207.
[11] Cf. Kant, *Critique of Judgment*, trans. J C Meredith (Oxford: Clarendon Press, 1982), part I, 58. 350.

that such knowledge has strong communal support, and points to a reality other than the merely subjective. Is there another way then to claim for aesthetics a rational, epistemic significance, a way that takes its judgments seriously as a source of universal truth? Yes, there is, but it is a way otherwise ill-suited to traditional modes of academic discourse. In recent decades, certain writers—mostly philosophers and poets—have devoted their attention to dismantling Enlightenment notions of artistic creation and interpretation in order to make room for a radically new form of "aesthetic consciousness". In this "newer new aesthetics", a work of art is understood not as a self-contained "thing" standing over against the subject, but rather as an "event", an effect of human history and experience. A work of art is shown to be a kind of processual interaction between the artist and the traditions in which he or she stands. It follows, in this more existentialist aesthetics, that notions of rationality must also be much broader—which is to say, much more holistic, much more human.

I will be suggesting in the course of this book that the affective and imaginative habits of mind illustrative of the artist, that the definitively human structure of aesthetic experience, that the experiential, intersubjective reasoning involved in aesthetic taste and judgment, however removed they may seem from the *techné* of religious dogmatics, might very well be the closest we can get to finding an heuristic parallel to the subtle mental processes described in Newman's writings on the nature of religious knowledge. I want further to state, and will try to show—though it is incidental to my project as a whole—that aesthetics can indeed be "epistemic", that it represents modes of rationality that play important roles in the determination of truth and meaning, that it provides a coherent framework for the understanding of certain psychical phenomena involved in the knowing process, religious or otherwise.

Still, a rationality of aesthetics alone is not a comprehensive enough schema to circumscribe the totality of Newman's complex theorising. I want to suggest therefore that aesthetics is but the particularisation of an even more subtle, more universal experience:

the experience of interpretation. In the existentialist aesthetics I will detail below, art is *Erlebniskunst*: i.e. what emerges from, represents and thus "speaks to" human experience. And because human experience is "always already" interpretative, art possesses the constitutional structure of interpretation. Interpretation is not something alien to the artwork, as if to suggest that a reading of it as one thing or another spoils its purity. This objectification of the purity and perfection of art was common to the Romantic aesthetics of Schiller and Schelling. As such it shares with the Enlightenment model a positivistic misconception about the finite nature of human rationality. I shall be arguing, to the contrary, that art is irreducibly interpretative, and that its truth-potential is therefore restricted to the limits inherent to interpretative description. I will go on to show that these limits, though keeping aesthetic transcendence strictly within the realm of human finitude, are nevertheless immensely productive.

But in order to accomplish all this, I will need to introduce another major thinker—this time from the twentieth century and from a tradition wholly removed from the more concrete formulations of British empiricism. There is only one writer I know of who in a systematic way has turned his attention to developing a rationality of aesthetics by means of first formulating a theory of interpretation. Hans-Georg Gadamer (b. 1900), like Newman born at the turn of his own century, and again like Newman living long enough to witness nearly its entire span, has had a profound influence in recent years on the nature and development of the human sciences. In his major work, *Truth and Method* (1960; first English version, 1975), Gadamer enters into dialogue with a variety of interpretation theories or "hermeneutics", especially those set forth by Schleiermacher (in biblical studies), Dilthey (in historical studies), and Heidegger (in ontological studies). In so doing, he takes recourse to several principles of aesthetics as they have been handed down, though in different ways, by Vico, Kant, Humboldt, Herder and Hegel, along with frequent excursions back to Plato and Aristotle. For reasons of this unique combination, that of a hermeneutical epistemology formulated in terms of a rationality of aesthetics, I have chosen Gadamer as a modern point of reference, and will allow his system to dictate my mode of entry into and critique of Newman's theory of religious knowledge.

Though Gadamer's work is much indebted to the sorts of traditions common to any late-twentieth century German philosopher, his contribution to philosophical hermeneutics is ground-breaking in its own right. In an age when philosophers are turning their backs on the ancients, Gadamer seeks to examine and in large part reclaim the whole Western development of aesthetic and hermeneutical thought since pre-Socratic times. His departure into this immense frame of history is guided by his desire to articulate and analyse the question of "truth" as it emerges in the experience of art. "My starting point", Gadamer writes,

> is that the historic human sciences [*Geisteswissenschaften*], as they emerged from German romanticism and became imbued with the spirit of modern science, maintained a humanistic heritage that distinguishes them from all other kinds of modern research and brings them close to other, quite different, extra-scientific experiences, and especially those proper to art.[12]

It is Gadamer's thorough if at times digressive explanation of this link between the human sciences and the "extra-scientific" experience of art that provides, I believe, an enlightening avenue into Newman's theory of religious knowledge. Conceptual delimitation cannot exhaust the content of art, any more than it can circumscribe all that happens when a religious experience or insight gives rise to free assent. For what is at stake in each is the acknowledgment that human responses to "the other" are a rough mix of the cognitive and

---

[12] Gadamer, *TM*, p. xvii.

the affective, of the psychological, volitional and—as we are becoming increasingly aware—the physiological. When analysed within the frame of Gadamer's hermeneutics, art is shown to be an interpretative form of expression in which concepts come together in a relatedness that outstrips the sum of its parts. So too religious knowledge: in Newmanian terms, such knowledge represents the summation of antecedent probabilities, each the effect of prior images, feelings, consensual opinions, analogous experiences and acts of trust, which in turn prompt that highly individualised *habitus*, the "illative sense" to integrate these bits into an act of assent greater than can be explained by its constituents.

That this Gadamerian "view", this aesthetic-hermeneutical mode of inquiry, is appropriate to Newman studies rests principally upon the coördination of two rather discontiguous worlds of thought: nineteenth-century British empiricism and twentieth-century German existentialism. I admit that such a proposal hardly lends itself to suggestion. There appears *prima facie* little in common between Newman's Oxonian Aristotelianism and Gadamer's Heidelbergian Platonism; between Newman's beloved Church Fathers and Gadamer's fondness for the pre-Socratics; between a publically Catholic dogmatician and a closet-Lutheran relativist. It may be helpful to know, therefore, that I am not alone in suggesting a correlation between the two.

FINDING PRECEDENT

Consider first the tag-line added by Nicholas Lash to the end of his introduction to the 1979 edition of Newman's *Grammar of Assent*. Lash entered the arena of Newman studies in 1975 with the publication of his doctoral thesis on Newman's theory of development.[13] Here he turns his attention to Newman's philosophy

---

[13] Cf. Nicholas Lash, *Newman on Development* (London: Sheed and Ward, 1975).

as a whole:

> Some years ago, J. M. Cameron claimed that 'Newman's
> *philosophical* originality has been underestimated'. For that
> underestimation to be corrected, certain widespread
> assumptions concerning what is to count as philosophical
> argument...had first to be called into question. In recent years,
> we have seen some rather fundamental shifts begin to take
> place in the assessment of the range and variety of modes of
> human rationality, shifts of which the widespread interest
> shown...in the 'critical theory' of the Frankfurt School and in
> works such as T. S. Kuhn's *Structure of Scientific Revolutions*
> and H.-G. Gadamer's *Truth and Method* may be taken as
> signals and indicators.[14]

Lash here announces the sort of paradigm shift in models of
rationality I am relying on to render an original and fruitful point of
entry into Newman's theory of religious knowledge. Consider further
the work of Thomas Norris in the 1977 publication of his doctoral
dissertation on Newman's theological method. Norris comments on
the same paradigm shift; but he reverses the direction, finding in
Newman's theoretical writings an anticipation of modern trends in
hermeneutical theory:

> We can conclude...that Newman seems to have anticipated by
> a long time the emergence of the contemporary problem of
> interpretation.   That problem is but the corollary to the
> discovery that every person in reasoning...is his own centre,
> and is not the mechanical instrument of a vague abstraction
> called reason. It has received excellent treatment at the hands
> of E. Betti, Fr. Lonergan, and H. G. Gadamer.[15]

Walter Kasper, theology professor at Tübingen, comments as well
on the remarkable prescience of Newman's insights into the kind of
interpretative stance appropriate to historical understanding, what

---

[14] Newman, *GA*, pp. 20-21. The reference to Cameron comes from *The Night Battle* (London:
Burns and Oates, 1962), p. 223.

[15] Thomas J Norris, *Newman and his Theological Method* (Leiden: E J Brill, 1977), p. 121.

Kasper calls "historical self-appropriation". Here again, it is the placement of Newman alongside thinkers not normally connected with him that is so striking:

> This method of historical dialectics (we have called it 'historical self-appropriation') was worked out by B. Pascal, J. E. Kuhn and J. H. Newman (in particular).....It bears a relation to the approach of contemporary hermeneutic inquiry as exemplified by H. G. Gadamer [sic].[16]

Consider finally the work of Bernard Lonergan. Though not a Newman scholar in the restricted sense, Lonergan has taken up and developed several of Newman's leading ideas within the broad framework of his transcendental epistemology. It was Newman's theory of development, for example, that led Lonergan to formulate theological method as a "normative pattern of recurrent and related operations yielding cumulative and progressive results".[17] It bears noting then that in a 1977 lecture entitled, "Theology and *Praxis*", Lonergan bears explicit if all too brief witness to the ideological connection between Newman and Gadamer. Speaking of the way rationality is exercised in the writings of Schopenhauer, Kierkegaard and Nietzsche, Lonergan unites them all under a common concern, *"praxis"*:

> [*Praxis*] is the kind of knowledge by which people live their lives. It is the kind of knowledge scientists, philosophers and theologians presuppose when they perform their specialised tasks. It is the knowledge of which Newman wrote in his *Grammar of Assent*, Polanyi in his *Personal Knowledge*, and Gadamer in his *Truth and Method*.[18]

---

[16] Walter Kasper, *Die Methoden der Dogmatik* (Munich: Kösel, 1966), pp. 40-41. Translation is mine.

[17] Bernard Lonergan, *Method in Theology* (London: 1972), p. 316.

[18] Bernard Lonergan, "Theology and *Praxis*", in *A Third Collection: Papers by Bernard Lonergan*, F Crowe, ed. (Mahwah, NJ: Paulist Press, 1985), p. 195.

But my thesis requires more than anecdotal support. It requires concrete proof. To this end I will turn my attention to four of Newman's key epistemological themes that together constitute his theory of religious knowledge: first principles, antecedent probabilities, historical development and the illative sense. For the purposes of critical analysis, I will set these four ideas alongside several aesthetic and hermeneutical principles culled from Gadamer's main work, *Truth and Method*. The Gadamerian themes have been chosen because I believe they represent near-equivalents to the basic constituents of Newman's epistemology. By means of comparison and contrast, then, I will attempt to show to what extent both Newman and Gadamer are thinking along the same lines, and to what extent they are not.

Before turning more explicitly to Newman's works, however, it will be essential to this study to take first a lengthy, but rather general look at Gadamer's project in order to outline what is meant when the terms aesthetics and hermeneutics are used, and to what extent they can be appropriated to access the various epistemological phenomena associated with Newman's theory of religious knowledge. I will thus begin with a three part introduction in which Gadamer's aesthetic and hermeneutical philosophies are presented in rudimentary form and, following that, critiqued.

In Part One I will return to Newman, but again by way of an introduction. Because he is only rarely acknowledged as a genuine philosopher, it seems appropriate to investigate from what sources Newman gathered his philosophical ideas. Thus, between the Gadamerian propaedeutic and my more constructive project of comparison and analysis that forms Part Two I have inserted a brief treatment of Newman's philosophical genealogy. To my knowledge—with one possible exception[19]—this has never been done before. I have not offered an exhaustive narrative, of course, but what I have managed to distil serves well to "break the ice" in the

[19] Cf. Edward Sillem's introduction to vol. I of *PN*, which Sillem edited.

conversation between Newman and the more philosophically trained Gadamer.

Finally, and by way of a conclusion, I will attempt to make a more synthetic response to the Newman-Gadamer dialogue. My aim will be to suggest in light of the foregoing not what can or cannot be known about God, but how one might go about knowing things about God were such a knowledge of God possible. The most formative assumption—or should I say *hope*?—of this project has been that if I can make aesthetic-hermeneutical inroads into an influential theory of how we come to form and develop religious knowledge, I will at the same time be able to expand the horizons of that theory into new, possibly fruitful ways of thinking about God, the world and ourselves. I will explore these possibilities at a more theoretical level by talking about three forms of religious knowing that I believe reflect well the epistemic implications of my Newman-Gadamer synthesis.

This thesis, for all intents and purposes, is working toward founding a method or way of proceeding in the study of religion that is drawn from the correspondence between Newman's philosophical thought and Gadamer's hermeneutical reclamation of the aesthetic tradition. Any explicit mention of this method however, will, except for a few concluding remarks, remain subsidiary to the more formative task of determining the degree of correspondence between the two. It will become obvious shortly that the nature of this correspondence is very broad. But then so are the horizons of thought Newman and Gadamer themselves put forth.

INTRODUCING GADAMER:

Reconstructing the Question of Aesthetics

My great longing is to learn to make those very incorrectnesses,
those deviations, remodellings, changes of reality, so that
my paintings may become, yes, untruth if you like—
but more true than the literal truth.

Vincent Van Gogh, *Letters to Theo*

Normally, aesthetics as a philosophical discipline is assigned to the analysis of concepts and the solution of problems that arise from the contemplation of aesthetic objects. Aesthetic objects in turn comprise all the objects of aesthetic experience. Hence it is only after aesthetic experience has been sufficiently characterised that one is able to say what is and what is not an aesthetic object. Aesthetic experience then is any event of sense perception we find agrees with our ideas of beauty, harmony, symmetry, order, etc., and which may or may not include sensual pleasure. My experience of a piece of music, for example, may or may not be aesthetic depending on whether or not it agrees with the way I conceptualise things like tonal harmony, beautiful rhythm, economy of form, and so on. To put this negatively, any aspect of human existence that is not involved in the experience of beauty—moral questions, questions of truth and meaning, of significance—will not normally enter into or alter the nature of aesthetic experience and is not considered to influence aesthetic judgment.

This in any case is the modern textbook definition of philosophical aesthetics. As John Hospers writes,

> An aesthetic judgment is not a judgment about the goodness or badness of something in any moral sense, nor is it a judgment about the truth or falsity of statements...Opposed views of the world are presented in the poems of Dante and Lucretius, but as aesthetic observers we do not have to choose between them; we can appreciate each view of life as it is presented without having to commit ourselves to either.[20]

JUDGMENTS OF TASTE

This now conventional definition of aesthetics derives in part from Kant's epistemology of the judgement of taste as found in the first part of his *Critique of Judgment* (1790). For Kant, judgments of taste cannot be expressed in logical terms, for they are neither cognitive acts nor object oriented. On the contrary, taste is "aesthetic" and "subjective"; i.e. it represents an internal awareness of the "feeling of pleasure" evoked in part by the senses, and in part by the "free play of the imagination" whenever something "tasteful" is encountered.[21] In classifying judgments of taste as aesthetic, therefore, Kant emphasizes that taste is a judgment whose "determining ground cannot be other than subjective".[22]

Having consigned the judgment of taste to the realm of subjectivity, Kant then sets himself the task of retrieving its legitimacy. He goes about this in the following way.[23] Judgments of

---

[20] John Hospers, "Problems of Aesthetics", in *The Encyclopedia of Philosophy* (New York: Macmillan and Free Press, 1967), p. 48.

[21] Kant, *The Critique of Judgement*, trans. J C Meredith (Oxford: Oxford University Press, 1982), § 9. 217. Section numbers here refer to Kant's own referencing system.

[22] Kant, *The Critique of Judgment*, § 1. 203.

[23] I am dependent for the following on Ted Cohen and Paul Guyer, *Essays in Kant's Aesthetics* (Chicago: University of Chicago Press, 1982), ch. 1.

taste, regardless of their subjectivity, may still claim a degree of universality. While the statement "x is beautiful" is deceptive in an objective sense, there is no deception in its intentionality, for saying "x is beautiful" is the only way to say what one wants to say about x *universally*. While the statement in itself may not have an objective contradictory, it is still a statement that can be *disagreed* with by others. Hence to ensure consensus, one must take pains to remove all possible obstacles that might inhibit a general agreement about x's beauty. Obstacles to such an agreement include, among other things, allowing sensual pleasure, priorly held concepts, and purposive interest to colour one's judgment. Thus to render aesthetic judgments free of any partiality, they must be made in a "detached" manner. Within this ascetic framework, judgments of taste are free to be universally representative:

> The judgment of taste, with its attendant consciousness of *detachment*, must involve a claim to validity for all [people], and must do so apart from the universality attached to Objects, i.e. there must be coupled with it a claim to subjective universality.[24]

It may seem like a contradiction in terms to speak of "subjective universality". But to render a judgment of taste in a form that assumes an objective referent indicates only that "impersonality" and "detachment" are necessary conditions for achieving the state of mind that in turn makes *intersubjective* validity possible. Once achieved, this intersubjective validity gives a judgment of taste its legitimacy as a universal judgment applicable to all.

Kant's theory as outlined above appears to reduce aesthetic experience to a merely subjective phenomenon. Enter Gadamer and his reconstruction of the classical tradition of aesthetics: does not Kant's reduction negate any possibility for the cognition of truth in the

---

[24] Kant, *The Critique of Judgment*, § 6. 212. Emphasis mine.

experience of art? Or to put the question positively, can art and the experiences it engenders possibly be something more than the product of subjective states? And if so, can it or they possibly issue forth in some sort of claim one would recognise as truthful? These are questions Gadamer wants to ask and, as we shall see, answer in the affirmative.

Gadamer begins with a positive appraisal of Kant's theory. By grounding the judgment of taste in an achieved state of intersubjective validity Kant has rightly aligned himself with the traditional notion of the *sensus communis*. And a "communal sense" is one of the elements from the aesthetic tradition Gadamer is desirous to rescue.

Gadamer's understanding of *sensus communis* should not be confused with the so-called "common sense philosophies" made popular in the eighteenth century by Hume and Reid, and in our own century by G E Moore. Gadamer links Kant's theory of aesthetic judgment to his aesthetic reappraisal by turning to Giambattista Vico (1668-1744) whose main work, *Scienza Nuova* anticipated, at least indirectly, several key ideas of the German idealists.[25] In his search for a coherent theory of first principles or *archai*, Vico rejects the Cartesian—and rationalist—notion of a conceptual intuition of "clear and distinct ideas" in favour of a *sensus communis* he sees at work in ancient Greek and Roman mentality, and upon which all subsequent reasoning has since been based. This original "sense of the community" was created not by logic but by archaic forms of human language "which burst forth from the human condition itself". Vico speculates that before articulate speech was invented, humans communicated using "a mute language of signs and physical objects having natural relations to the ideas they wished to express".[26] This

---

[25] Several attempts have been made, unsuccessfully, to link Vico's writings to Hegel. See, for example, Benedetto Croce, "An Unknown Page from the Last Months of Hegel's Life", trans. J Hillesheim and E Caserta, *The Personalist*, 45 (1964): 344-45, and 351. Croce's interest in seeing Vico as the Italian Hegel is the basis for his study *La Filosofia di Giambattista Vico* (1911), translated by Collingwood. Croce invented an imaginary conversation set during Hegel's last days, in which Hegel is introduced to Vico's thought by a visiting Neapolitan scholar.

mute language, he suggests, was the primary mode of representation for the ancient mind. When ancient Greeks or Romans thought about something, in other words, they were able to do so because already in place in their minds were readily intelligible, though wordless, patterns of meaning. As conventional forms of intelligibility, these patterns were passed on from generation to generation, later taken up into articulate discourse, and now in modern times are what enable judgments to take place.

The *sensus communis*, therefore, does not depend upon a fixed set of maxims, nor is it itself a set of consciously formed beliefs. Rather, it is of a people, a community, and is rooted in shared ways of feeling, experiencing and symbolising meaning in the world. Gadamer compares it to Aristotle's *phronesis*, where practical knowledge of concrete particulars rather than abstract universals legislates action, and for which "everything depends upon the circumstances".[27] One acquires *sensus communis*, Gadamer argues, by committing oneself to one's community, allowing oneself to absorb its traditions and experiences, and later, reflecting on those experiences in the light of one's own.[28] *Sensus communis* is thus a *praxis*, to usurp Lonergan's rubric, which helps us make simple judgments between right and wrong, true and false, beautiful and ugly, and so on.[29] It is "common" because of the social and political elements involved in the handing on of knowledge, and it is a "sense" in the way it functions, namely as providing access to a "concrete" knowledge of essences—i.e. as a way "to the things themselves".

And, Gadamer contines, what is important about the *sensus communis* is its relationship to real, everday circumstances. Its

---

[26] Giambattista Vico, *The New Science*, trans. T G Bergin, M H Fisch (New York: Doubleday Books, 1961), pp. 3-4.

[27] Gadamer, *TM*, p. 23.

[28] For a summary of Gadamer's comments on *sensus communis*, see Joel Weinsheimer, *Gadamer's Hermeneutics: A Reading of Truth and Method* (New Haven: Yale University Press, 1985), pp. 72-80.

[29] Gadamer calls this cognitive function "tact" after its use by Helmholz to describe a certain mode of knowing in the sciences. Cf. *TM*, pp. 16f.

judgments are not founded upon universals, but upon "things that all men see daily before them, things that hold an entire society together, things that are concerned both with truths and statements, ways and forms of expressing statements."[30]

Kant, on the other hand, in the process of investigating the foundations of taste discovered an *a priori* element lying beyond the kind of circumstantial universality seen in Vico's notion of *sensus communis*. This insight, asserts Gadamer, "gave birth" to his *Critique of Judgment*, and informs its entire system. Though it was Kant's ostensible aim to provide only a detailed description of aesthetic taste and judgment, this was not the essay's only result. In Gadamer's words, Kant's third *Critique* yields "a critique of critique" itself, i.e. a concern with the internal development of an *a priori*, universal subjectivity, a subjectivity of a sort that renders judgments of taste not only possible but binding.[31]

And Kant's meta-critique is partly correct, says Gadamer. He is correct in supposing that the universal value of the beautiful cannot be derived from empirical principles alone. Judgments of taste are not demonstrable in the same way scientific propositions are. It is written into the very fabric of aesthetic taste to transcend empirical conventions and grounds of judgment, otherwise it would not stand the test of time. As Gadamer's outline of the history of the concept shows, in subjective judgments of taste it is not only particular preferences but also "supra-empirical norms" that are operative.[32] But then this means that aesthetic judgments of taste must affirm two things: when they are only empirically grounded they are not universal; and if they are to be universal, they must find some non-empirical ground on which to stand. And both of these Kant's theory does affirm—hence the rub. For Kant, to make sense of a non-empirical universality that is still strictly subjective, as all judgments

[30] Gadamer, *TM*, p. 27. Gadamer cites here the German Pietist, Ötinger, who himself relies on the British philosopher, Lord Shaftesbury and the latter's defence of the *sensus communis*.
[31] Gadamer, *TM*, pp. 39-42.
[32] Gadamer, *TM*, p. 40.

of taste are, one must assume its legitimating ground to be subjective *a priori*. And this, says Gadamer, rules out from the start all real, existential contact with the aesthetic object; it rules out a real encounter with *the truth* of the thing:

> The price [Kant] pays for this legitimation of criticism in the area of taste is that he denies that taste has any significance as knowledge. It is a *subjective* principle to which he reduces *sensus communis*. In it nothing is known of the objects that are judged as beautiful, but it is stated only that *a priori* there is a feeling of pleasure connected with them in the subjective consciousness.[33]

In this book I am concerned with knowledge, hence I must take Gadamer's criticism to heart. He points out that the key to the problem is Kant's a-historical understanding and use of *sensus communis*. When Kant calls taste the true *sensus communis*,[34] he no longer has in mind "the great moral and political tradition" of the original concept as used by Vico.[35] In fact, Vico's notion is rejected outright as having anything to do with aesthetic taste. For Kant, *sensus communis* is based on "concepts" instead of the pure subjectivity of "feeling" that grounds judgments of aesthetic taste. Indeed in Kant's theory, feeling itself functions as a concept, albeit the mother of all aesthetic concepts, and that which is necessary to making aesthetic judgments possible.[36] Kant is thus forced to abstract taste from any and all empirical elements in order to found it upon what arises subjectively—"pleasure"—when the "free-play" of our cognitive faculties, and only such faculties, is stimulated by an aesthetic object. Its universality is thus negatively determined as something divorced from real life, instead of positively as based on the empirical grounds of what actually creates and sustains the

---

[33] Gadamer, *TM*, p. 40. Emphasis added.
[34] Kant, *Critique of Judgment*, § 20. 238.
[35] Gadamer, *TM*, p. 41.
[36] Cf. Paul Guyer, "Pleasure and Society in Kant's Theory of Taste", in *Essays in Kant's Aesthetics*, p. 24.

sensus communis.[37]

So while Kant has correctly given the judgment of taste its proper social orientation—the need for consensual agreement—he has divorced this social factor from, among other things, existential, historical and linguistic influences, all of which are inextricably bound to judgments of taste—in fact, to judgments of any kind.

Gadamer himself has something more comprehensive in mind. For once they are set within the traditional Viconian notion of the *sensus communis*, aesthetic judgments of taste become a type of "sense" incorporating a wide range of rational acts, and by which we attain to a real knowledge of things. Aesthetic taste, says Gadamer, is "an element of civic and moral being".[38] By this he means that the condition rendering aesthetic judgment operative includes a real connection between an art-work and the community that receives and interprets the work. The experience of art is thus more than an encounter with an individual artist's creativity. It is an event that occurs within the larger context of a surrounding community and its inherited, intuitive norms of taste.

BILDUNG AND SELF-FORMATION

Gadamer may be slightly off the mark here with his polemic against Kant's theory of taste, for recent studies have tried to bring to light connections between Kant's aesthetics and his theory of morals, the latter of which embodies a more socio-cultural emphasis.[39]

---

[37] This is why, for example, Kant prefers natural over artistic beauty. Natural beauty possesses no clear content, and manifests a purely non-conceptual instantiation of taste. No cognition need be involved. As he writes, "Now I willingly admit that the interest in the beautiful of art...gives no evidence at all of a habit of mind attached to the morally good, or even inclined that way. But, on the other hand, I do maintain that to take an immediate interest in the beauty of nature...is always a mark of a good soul". Cf. Kant, *Critique of Judgment*, § 42. 298-299.

[38] Gadamer, *TM.*, p. 31.

[39] Cf. Paul Crowther, *The Kantian Sublime* (Oxford: Clarendon Press, 1989). In addition, see Ted Cohen, "Why Beauty is a Symbol of Morality", in T Cohen, *Essays in Kant's Aesthetics*, pp. 221-36.

Regardless, Gadamer's intention in reacting to Kant is to embrace a traditional theory of aesthetic judgment that at the same time makes room for the cognition of "truth". He does this in part, as we have seen, by subsuming aesthetic taste under the notion of the *sensus communis*. But by far his more detailed argument involves underlining aesthetic judgment with the notion of *Bildung*, "education", or more accurately, "self-formation".

German has two words for "education": *Bildung* and *Erziehung*. Whereas the latter emphasises the process of education itself, the former stresses more its result and thus accesses a wider application. Besides "to educate", *bilden*, from which the substantive is derived, may also mean "to form, shape, fashion, develop, cultivate" and "broaden the mind". This extension of meaning is demonstrated by the word's many linguistic relatives: *Bild* [form, picture], *Abbild* [copy], *ausbilden* [to cultivate], *Nachbild* [reproduction], *Vorbild* [exemplar], *Urbild* [original], *Gebilde* [structure] and, most significantly, *Einbildung* [imagination]. Goethe's *Wilhelm Meister*, for example, has been called a *Bildungsroman*, an "educational novel", because its protagonist experiences a series of encounters that transforms him into a "beautiful soul". And Schleiermacher's 1799 "Speeches on Religion", addressed to his "cultured [*gebildeten*] despisers" of religion, develops an argument for religious consciousness as that which alone fulfils the human desire for "highest culture" [*höchste Bildung*].[40]

Gadamer plays on this link between *Bildung* and the soul or consciousness, and makes it a leading concept in his analysis of the structural formation of aesthetic judgment. Much like the Hellenic notion of *paideia* on which it is modelled, *Bildung* details an interest in education and enculturation that supersedes any interest in the attainment of certain knowledge. Its concern is not a final,

---

[40] Cf. Terry Foreman, *Religion as the Heart of Humanistic Culture: Schleiermacher as Exponent of Bildung in the Speeches of Religion of 1799* (Ann Arbor: University Microfilms, 1977).

irrevocable understanding of "truth" but rather "an awareness of different possibilities of coping with the world, of different life-options...of new modes of self-description".[41] *Bildung* represents a worldview that celebrates that other, more contentious Kantian imperative, "dare to think". It disrupts the fixed generalities of hypostatic universalisation in favour of the flux and fluidity of the historical process. From the point of view of *Bildung*, what is important is less the possession of absolute truth than our own development toward a more holistic self-understanding, and hence toward an understanding of the world of art as expressive of the human condition.

According to Gadamer, the person who is *gebildet* or "spiritually cultured" is one who has moved beyond the narrow confines of private interests to take up instead the interests of the community to which he or she belongs; and beyond that to adopt an interest in world history, cultures and languages. This is all with a view to reflecting that exposure back upon the self, to re-defining the self and its limits over against the "otherness" it encounters in its ever widening frames of reference. "It is clear", writes Gadamer in summary, "that it is not alienation as such but the return to oneself, which presumes a prior alienation, that constitutes the essence of *Bildung*".[42]

The opposite condition, the state of being *ungebildet*, defines by contrast a certain parochial narrow-mindedness toward what is unfamiliar. It is the state of mind of the detached, isolated individual who eschews all forms of communal involvement, who considers his or her own views alone to be sufficient. "Whoever abandons himself to his own particularity", writes Gadamer, "is *ungebildet*....He cannot turn his gaze from himself toward something universal from which his own particular being is determined in measure and proportion".[43] Which is to say that *Bildung* requires a sacrifice of

---

[41] Gadamer, *TM*, pp. 156-57.
[42] Gadamer, *TM*, p. 15.
[43] Gadamer, *TM*, p. 13.

self-assertive views and opinions in order to make room for more universal, more proportionate forms of consciousness. This sacrifice preserves a certain tactfulness within consciousness that allows for a greater measure of flexibility in one's understanding of the world and oneself.

One hears shades of Hegel here, of course. And indeed, in describing the process of *Bildung* Gadamer relies heavily on Hegelian dialectic, and particularly the notion of *Aufhebung* or "self-overcoming". Hegel's *Bildungstheorie* includes the assertion of a dialectic between familiarity and otherness that then yields a broader, more universal perspective. The "sensitive soul" becomes *gebildet*, according to Hegel, when it is forced to confront its own limits in the face of the alienating objective reality that surrounds and supports it. This felt-alienation then fuels the desire to transform the unknown into the familiar. This is done through a projection of the self, the self searching for what it already knows in otherwise foreign surroundings, whereupon a "reversal in consciousness" is experienced—the known unlocks the unknown, and horizons of understanding are moved to a higher level. In Hegelian terms, then, *Bildung* defines the limitations of one's own perspective, only then to surpass those limits in the effort "to acquire a new horizon".[44]

But Gadamer is dissatisfied with Hegel's account when the "great Gymnasium director" reveals his "classicist's prejudice" by suggesting that it is particularly the study of classical literature that most readily effects the transformation of *Bildung*.[45] An education in Greco-Roman aesthetics, says Hegel, best initiates the self-alienation that is the first step toward a *gebildete*, integrated self-understanding. For whoever would study the world of antiquity should come to experience at what great remove he or she is from its beauty of language, culture and virtue: a conflictual experience that yields a drive to expand one's consciousness until it realises within itself such fullness and depth. Gadamer, however, though fond of the classics

---

[44] Gadamer, *TM*, p. 317.
[45] Gadamer, *TM*, p. 15.

does not share Hegel's prejudice, and thus balks at the particularity of his application. Yet he adds that "the basic idea is correct....To seek one's own in the alien, to become at home in it, is the basic movement of spirit, whose being is only return to itself from what is other".[46] The Hegelian concept of *Bildung* has revealed a fundamental dynamism of human spirit, says Gadamer. Namely this: that once the human psyche is exposed to forms of human value and meaning more genuinely universal than its own, it is restless until it learns to expand itself to the same proportions.

Having thus set the aesthetic concepts of taste and judgment within the traditional notions of the *sensus communis* and *Bildung*, Gadamer is satisfied he has restored them to their "original breadth". It remains to be said that despite their opposition to an objective knowledge of facts, Gadamer claims that *sensus communis* and *Bildung*, as illustrative of the natural movement of consciousness toward increasingly expansive, universal forms of understanding, represent much more than an education into pluralism—Richard Rorty's "potential infinity of vocabularies".[47] On the contrary, by means of his aesthetic reconstruction Gadamer wants to assert as close a connection as possible between a community-based *Bildung* and a knowledge toward which one can be resolute, and of which one can be certain. For when one allows oneself to be formed by the *sensus communis*, and on the strength of that formation to assimilate into one's horizon of understanding the understandings of other cultures, languages, peoples and places, one then possesses a more ecumenical, and thus more epistemicaly effective form of subjectivity; i.e. one's ability to subsume particulars under universals is more acute, more "tactful". This in Gadamer's estimation is a strong foundation for knowledge, a platform of cognitive support from which one may make reasonable truth-claims, and thus live in the

---

[46] Gadamer, *TM*, p. 15.
[47] Cf. Richard Rorty, *Philosophy and the Mirror of Nature* (Princeton: Princeton University Press, 1979), p. 367.

light of them.

And yet, because the *sensus communis* and *Bildung* are elements of "social and moral being",[48] and thus historical, processual phenomena—i.e. definitively human phenomena—the aesthetic judgments they effect lack all the usual criteria for objectivity. In these more intuitive, more affective forms of rationality, there is little in the way of critical distance established between the judging subject and the aesthetic object, for each is caught up in pre-given forms of mediation that both enable and limit the cogency of interpretation. A fuller description of this tension is to follow, and thus I will need to demonstrate how Gadamer resolves it before considering it an apt schema for my investigation into Newman's theory of religious knowledge.

---

[48] Gadamer, *TM*, p. 31.

INTRODUCING GADAMER:

Reconstructing the Question of Hermeneutics

In the beginning there was a river.
The river became a road
and the road branched out
to the whole world.

Ben Okri, *The Famished Road*

We have it straight from Aristotle that living a good life is difficult. The state of character concerned with wise "deliberation" [*bouleuesthai*] and making proper "choices" [*prohaireseis*] is described in the *Nicomachean Ethics* as a narrow "mean" between two wide, clearly marked paths of vice, each of which is well-travelled. "To miss the mark is easy; to hit it difficult".[49] Martin Heidegger makes a similar comparison when he describes inauthentic existence as one that "tends to make things easy for itself",[50] is "tranquillised" into thinking that "everything is within its reach".[51] As an alternative Heidegger proposes a "hermeneutics of facticity"

---

[49] Aristotle, *Nicomachean Ethics*, bk. II.6, 1106b.
[50] Cf. Heidegger, "Phänomenologische Interpretationen zu Aristotles: Einführung in die Phänomenologische Forschung", *Gesamtausgabe* (Frankfurt: Klostermann, 1985), vol. 1, pp. 108-10.
[51] Heidegger, *Being and Time*, trans. Macquarrie and Robinson (New York: Harper & Row, 1962), p. 223.

that seeks to "restore factical existence to its original difficulty". A hermeneutics of facticity tries to bring to light the constraints put upon human understanding by living within the confines of time; to articulate "the abyss, the play, the uncanny" aspects of human rationality; to promote, in John Caputo's phrase, an "owning up to the fix we are in".[52]

In the hermeneutical analysis of the "fix we are in", the outlines of which I will be tracing in this chapter, one sees the phenomenon of the consciousness of human facticity move to the centre of philosophical interest. Hermeneutics seizes upon the insight that the appropriation of human meaning and truth is not directed by an objectively perceiving, transcendent *ego* articulating itself in timeless statements, but rather by a consciousness that grows in the awareness of its situatedness in time and place. Because of the *a priori* nature of this "temporal-regionality", it is bound to project itself into the interpretative process, to condition its results, and to limit its claim to universality.

But as Gadamer wants to demonstrate, despite placing severe restrictions on what can or cannot be held as universally true, human situatedness is what sets the interpretational dynamic in motion in the first place. Human finitude is the condition that makes an understanding of truth possible. Which raises a critical question: for if the temporal-regional world that limits human cognition projects itself into every interpretation as both its confining medium *and* the condition of its possibility, how is interpretative understanding ever to bring to maturity results that pass the test of time? How can interpretations inextricably linked to the here and now claim to speak for all times and places? In a more scientific or methodological model, knowledge is transferred linearly from one logical step to the next without reference to the situatedness of the knower. The axioms of geometry, the laws of physics and the properties of chemical

---

[52] John Caputo, *Radical Hermeneutics: Repetition, Deconstruction and the Hermeneutic Project* (Bloomington: Indiana University Press, 1987), p. 6.

compounds are all considered to be permanently fixed truths, irrevocable, and uninfluenced by the people who formulated them. But hermeneutical reasoning, which Gadamer insists is at work in every form of human understanding, science included, works more circuitously, moving back and forth as a kind of conversation between interpreter and interpretand, each partner in the dialogue reaching ever further into the subject matter, each melding into each in what Gadamer calls the "fusion of horizons". How then can we apply the concept "knowledge" to the yield of hermeneutical reasoning if its parameters are so non-objective, so meta-logical? How can Gadamer speak of truth if it is not a truth for all times and places?

SEEING, PROJECTING AND FUSING

To answer this query requires rehearsing several key ideas in hermeneutical philosophy. I have already said that it is a principal aim of Gadamer's work in *Truth and Method* to deconstruct the Enlightenment's model of "objectivity". Primary to Gadamer's vision as a whole is the conviction that truth can only be reached via "the totality of human experience".[53] This rules out the hope that, once discovered through the application of scientific method, truth can be enjoyed in an undistorted, unbiased state. On the contrary, Gadamer seriously questions the modernist assumption that scientific methodologies provide direct access to objective "facts". In a hermeneutical model of rationality, there are no *facta bruta*, no things-in-themselves beyond temporal and spatial ordering, no naked essences, no bare quiddities that are not "always already" [*immer schon*] coloured, construed and sometimes contorted by the subjects who perceive them. It is basic to philosophical hermeneutics that perception is always already interpretation, seeing always a "seeing-

---

[53] Gadamer, "The Universality of the Hermeneutical Problem", in *Philosophical Hermeneutics* (Berkeley: University of California Press, 1976), p. 179.

as".

Gadamer is optimistic about this description, however. He is not
calling for an end to philosophy and metaphysics, as some of his
French colleagues have done. The finitude that limits human reason
is the very essence of what it means to be human, but it does not
necessarily preclude the ability to "see what is there". In fact, without
it there would be no "seeing" in the first place. The negative inference
is this: "seeing" is never a "pure seeing". Rather, it is always already
"prejudiced" by the very things that make it possible. But far from
rendering the world meaningless, Gadamer sees this prejudical forestructuring of perception brimming with creative potential. He
explains:

> Even perception conceived as an adequate response to a
> stimulus would never be a mere mirroring of what is there.
> For it always remains an understanding of something as
> something. All understanding-*as* is an articulation of what is
> there, in that it looks away from, looks at, sees together as, and
> so on...Equally it is led by its expectations to read in what is not
> there at all.
>
> ...Pure seeing and pure hearing are dogmatic abstractions
> which artificially reduce phenomena. Perception, in other
> words, always involves meaning.[54]

For this reason, Gadamer questions methodologies of any kind
whenever they base themselves on the Enlightenment model of
detached, unprejudiced objectivity. Such objectivity is a myth, and a
destructive one at that. For the clarion call of "detached objectivity"
is all too easily exploited, too readily a mask worn by people hiding
their wills to power. As I will examine below in greater detail,
Gadamer is convinced that scientific methods, as well as science-
based methods of interpretation, tend to disregard some of the more
basic acts of human perception and understanding, acts that are so
deeply a part of us they slip through the grasp of methodical

---

[54] Gadamer, *TM*, pp. 81-82.

representation.

Gadamer's assumption, then, is that modern methods of explanation in whatever field lose sight of the pre-given historicality of human existence, the rootedness in time and place that is an inextricable part of being human. Methodological consciousness seeks to abstract the more specifiable moments of human experience from their proper context of world-engagement in order to submit them to preconceived rules of analysis. It does so because it assumes that our human mode of being has the potential to distance itself from Being, to transcend the flux of time and reduce all materiality to a thematic essence. Gadamer says this Cartesian presupposition is false. He agrees with his mentor, Heidegger, who determines that humans exist always in a primary state of "belongingness" [Zugehörigkeit] to Being. As Heidegger has phrased it, human existence is "thrown" into the world at birth and is "ever on the way toward death".[55] In between these two existential moments there is the more ontological moment of a deep connectedness to life that cannot be overcome; to the world that is both a product of our interpretative projections, and the very substance that makes those projections possible. Human being in Heideggerian parlance is a "being-in-the-world", a Dasein ["being-there"] conditioned by history, by time, by Being itself.

Gadamer has made much capital out of this definition. He argues that in epistemological terms the deep connection humans have with Being suggests "a coordination of all knowing activity with what is known"[56] such that "the knower is not standing over against a situation that he merely observes but...is directly affected by what he sees".[57] This is so because what we see, what we turn our interpretative attention toward, is a part of the same world we inhabit. It is a product of the same temporal-regionality that has

[55] Cf. Heidegger, Being and Time, pp. 172-224.
[56] Gadamer, TM, p. 232.
[57] Gadamer, TM, p. 280.

shaped our own being-in-the-world. Understanding is therefore a projection of ourselves onto what is to be understood; and rightly so, for it and we are of the same mode of being. Which is another way of saying that all understanding is, at some level, self-understanding.

Self-understanding in Gadamer's definition is grounded by an understanding of the way humans exist in the world generally, i.e. of their proper orientation as *Dasein* in its fundamental "openness" to reality. What is therefore known in self-understanding is a form of "ready-to-hand" knowledge, to use the Heideggerian phrase;[58] which is to say a form of knowledge that opens up the realm of practical knowing, a knowing through experience, a knowing that is not learned as one learns a geometrical theorem, but is gained as a "skill" simply by living and reflecting on one's life. Gadamer takes his cues here from Aristotle—as had Newman before him—and Aristotle's doctrine of *phronesis*, as I mentioned above. *Phronesis* details a situational form of knowing that takes into account the formational nature of life's experiences, and that possesses a dynamism and flexibility made possible by the fundamental temporal-regional relationship between subject and object.[59]

Gadamer tells us, famously, that the outcome of this fundamental "openness" of human being to its world, at least *in posse*, is a "fusion of horizons";[60] a metaphorical rendering of what we would now call "consciousness-raising". But first: what is a "horizon" [*Horizont*]? A "horizon" is a subjective realm of awareness that borders on two distinct but related fronts: the historical and the linguistic. Both our "thrownness" into history as our temporal-regional medium, and thus into a whole array of traditions (religious, political, social, etc.) that inform our values and actions, *and* our "thrownness" into

---

[58] Heidegger, *Being and Time*, p. 69.

[59] Gadamer, *TM*, pp. 41f.

[60] Cf. Gadamer, *TM*, pp. 269f; and Georgia Warnke, *Gadamer: Hermeneutics, Tradition and Reason* (Stanford: Stanford University Press, 1987), pp. 69, 82, 90, 103, 107-08, 137, 146, 169; Weinsheimer, pp. 183-84, 210, 211, 251; Anthony Thiselton, *The Two Horizons* (Grand Rapids: Eerdmans, 1980), pp. 10-16, and 293f.

language (or for some, languages) that structures our patterns of thought, and in so doing limits them to certain pre-given constructs of meaning, together form the infrastructure of consciousness by means of which we come to understand ourselves and the world around us. This historico-linguistic framework, in Gadamerian terms, acts as our interpretative "horizon"—i.e. as a forestructured network of self-understanding that frames all subsequent understanding of what is outside ourselves.

The metaphor of "horizon", with its long history in German literature, articulates well both the finitude and seemingly infinite potential of human understanding. One can speak of a "narrowness of horizon" or an "expansion of horizon", each to epistemological advantage. Or even, as Gadamer reminds us, of a person with "no horizon" who "does not see far enough and hence overvalues what is nearest".[61] But horizons are not fixed; at least they are not meant to be. They are products of our primordial openness to Being, hence are transformed as time and experience bring new visions of reality. The *modus operandi* of this transformation, thus, is "fusion". A truly new experience is, in Gadamer's argument, a "fusion" of the subject's present horizon with that of the object(s) of experience in such a way that a larger, more perceptive horizon results. This "fusion of horizons", in turn, expands one's awareness of the world; it increases the possibilities for new experiences, and thus further expanses of understanding. For in the fusion we learn new descriptive vocabularies with which we are able to ask better questions of "the other"; and so we engage ourselves more fruitfully in ever more deeply understood conversation. Moreover, this processual development of understanding in the "fusion of horizons" is never-ending, says Gadamer, and thus ever-leading to deeper penetrations into self- and world-knowledge. With all due respect to the theological work of John Hick and Wolfhart Pannenberg, the latter of whom Gadamer acknowledges as "helpful" but ultimately

---

[61] Gadamer, *TM*, p. 269.

mistaken,[62] there is no final "eschatological verification" for which we must wait. Time and the transformation of Being will forever bring new experiences that alter, perhaps negate the understandings that arose from previous ones.

ARTISTIC MIMESIS

The arena in which the "fusion of horizons" is most clearly articulated, states Gadamer, is that of art. Here Gadamer synthesises his hermeneutical ontology with an interest in epistemological themes derived from (mostly) Western traditions of philosophical aesthetics. Unlike Kant, he does not subordinate the mimetic, representational form of aesthetic interpretation to conceptual thought. Art—and here Gadamer intends all the arts: fine, literary and performance[63]—is always already conceptual as it stands. Art represents the world; it draws the essence of worldly things into form [ins Gebilde] and structures, even heightens their being.[64] More importantly, art is representative *for* the world;[65] as art gives expression to reality, it also speaks out on its behalf. As Gadamer puts it, "Reality is defined as what is untransformed, and art as the raising up of this reality into its truth".[66] It is the truth of art that speaks to us in the aesthetic experience; that interprets us even as we are interpreting it.

---

[62] Cf. Gadamer, *PH*, p. 36, where Gadamer states, significantly, that the critical different between his work and Pannenberg's is that for the latter "the 'practical purpose' of all universal historical conceptions has its fixed point in the absolute historicity of the Incarnation". While Gadamer does not dispute this claim, it is clear in distancing himself from it he questions its veracity.

[63] In contrast to Gadamer, Hegel assesses the arts on a sliding scale according to the greater or lesser degree they utilize spatial and material dimensions. Music was the highest of the arts next to poetry, the latter being the end point of Spirit's inward journey, the least materially oriented. Architecture, for obvious reasons, was considered the most primitive. Cf. Stephen Bungay, *Beauty and Truth* (Oxford: Clarendon Press, 1984), pp. 97 *et passim*.

[64] Cf. Gadamer, *TM*, pp. 73-90, and the chapter entitled, "Transformation into Structure and Total Mediation", pp. 99-107.

[65] Gadamer, *TM*, pp. 99f.

[66] Gadamer, *TM*, p. 102.

This raises the question of the differences between art and non-art, good art and kitsch. Surely not all that passes for art is to be thought of as "raising up reality into its truth". Not all art heightens the essence of things and draws it into some sort of cognizable structure. Unfortunately, Gadamer's exploration of this important question is incomplete. His aim is not to provide evaluative criteria.[67] Rather, he seeks to retrieve art from its dismissal as non-cognitive, and to purify its stance as epistemic. When Kant limited the province of knowledge to pure natural science, he set art outside that realm. Art thus came to be equated with the unreal. "Where art rules", says Gadamer in summary of the Kantian position, "the laws of beauty are in force and the boundaries of reality are transcended".[68] When Schiller, for example, urged his readers to educate themselves aesthetically, he proposed to make them citizens of an "ideal realm" in which aesthetic perfection reigns, not of the real world with all its "ambiguities". Gadamer strongly opposes this view. And to prove his position he draws on Aristotle, Gestalt psychology and phenomenology to show that aesthetic perception is not as "pure" as Schiller might have thought. It is instead an "understanding" that involves at all levels personal, interpretative reasonings.

Gadamer synthesises his findings with a reappropriation of the classical aesthetic notion of mimesis.[69] Mimesis is more than mere imitation, he says. When taken from the Aristotelian tradition (as opposed to the Platonic), it assumes the more cognitively oriented meaning of "representation", which in turn evokes the response of "recognition". When applied to art, this can be demonstrated in three ways. First, art is representative of ideas, not just empirical forms and shapes. Even highly creative art like Cubism or Expressionism

---

[67] For criticism of this lack in Gadamer's project, see E.D. Hirsch, *Validity in Interpretation* (New Haven: Yale University Press, 1967); and Emilio Betti, *Die Hermeneutik als allgemeine Methodik der Geisteswissenschaften* (Tübingen: JCB Mohr, 1962).

[68] Gadamer, *TM*, p. 74.

[69] Cf. Warnke, *Gadamer*, pp. 56-64.

contains real ideational content, proposes ways of looking at reality, offers "horizons" with which one may grapple, even fuse. Art is a kind language, asserts Gadamer, and is thus only rightly "encountered" and understood when one takes the time to listen to what it has to say.[70]

Second, it is the aim of art to highlight certain hidden aspects of the things it represents; "concrete" aspects that in coming out of concealment sometimes "shock" us, but always leave us better informed as to the totality of Being they help constitute. The "truth" of art, i.e. its mimetic disclosure of Being, challenges us to change our conventional ways of thinking, to expand our all-too-familiar horizons of understanding. Art seeks to add an "additional something"[71] to our finite perspectives: it may not be easily assimilated, nor ought it always to be so; but we are always in some way improved for having taken the time to consider its merit.

And third, in our response to the art-work we not only learn new things about the object represented, we learn more about ourselves as well. Like Plato's doctrine of *anamnesis*, there emerges from our seemingly infinite store of *memoranda* a "recognition" of something that pertains to self-understanding; we recognise in the artistic portrayal of reality something real about ourselves, something of the "truth that we are".[72] But for Gadamer, the anamnestic movement of "recognition" that art effects is not, as it was for Plato, a call from our higher selves to remember our true mode of transcendence; it is rather a call that wells up from within and calls us toward the existential structures of our finitude. When Heidegger writes at length on Van Gogh's painting of a dirty pair of peasant shoes, it is

---

[70] Cf. Gadamer, "The Speechless Image", in *RB*, pp. 83-91, in which Gadamer calls art a "speechless *language*"; and compare *RB*, p. 93: "If an artist could express himself in words, he would not wish to create and would not need to give form to his ideas. At the same time, it is inevitable that language, the universal communicative element that supports and holds together our human community, constantly awakens in the artist a need to communicate and express himself".

[71] Gadamer, *RB*, p. 34.

[72] Gadamer, *PH*, p. 16.

interpretation, but rather the knowledge of *praxis* that is recalled in and through the aesthetic experience. "From the dark opening of the worn insides of the shoes", he writes, "the toilsome tread of the worker stares forth":

> In the stiffly rugged heaviness of the shoes there is the accumulated tenacity of her slow trudge through the far-spreading and ever-uniform furrows of the field swept by a raw wind. On the leather lie the dampness and richness of the soil. Under the soles slides the loneliness of the field-path as evening falls. In the shoes vibrates the silent call of the earth, its quiet gift of the ripening grain and its unexplained self-refusal in the fallow desolation of the wintry field.[73]

This is more than interpretation *in abstracto*; it is a recollection of long walks along country paths, of pauses to watch tireless workers scything the hay, and the sensual pleasure, upon returning home again, of removing one's heavy, mud-encrusted shoes. It is the product of "a fusion of horizons"; the naively agrarian horizon of a 1950's German professor of philosophy enfolding itself around the horizon of a raving Dutchman in the 1880's with a genius for the fields.

By "truth in art", therefore, Gadamer means that in the artistic act of representation, as well as in the interpretative act of recognition, some disregarded aspect of human experience, some long-forgotten piece of self-understanding, has been re-discovered, separated out from others, illuminated, enshrouded with past memories and future expectations, and finally brought into artistic expression by being given form, shape, colour and texture in the work of art. When put in these terms, Gadamer's conception has affinities with Heidegger's account of truth as *aletheia* or disclosure: i.e. it marks an uncovering of some aspect of the world and/or our self-understandings otherwise occluded by familiarity or "forgetfulness".[74] In the artistic rendering

---

[73] Heidegger, "On the Origin of the Work of Art", in *Poetry, Language, Thought,* trans. A Hofstadter (San Francisco: Harper & Row, 1971), pp. 33-34.

of reality, nothing depicted is left uninterpreted; nothing is presented as "brute fact". Some one or several aspects of the thing are crystallised out of the infinite nexus of historical relationships that condition it, and are revealed, as Gadamer writes, "in the heightened truth of [their] being".[75] Artistic representation is thus an ideational representation of truth in the sense that it releases its subject matter from a contingent mode of being. The kind of truth art presents, therefore, cannot be strictly empirical; but it is no less the truth for its lack of verifiability. It is simply truth presented from another angle, that of representation and interpretation.

Art, then, does not present its "truth" in the same way a straightforward proposition does. Both can be said to be "meaningful",[76] but they are not meaningful in the same way. Because art is representative, and it is inherent to the nature of representation to be indirect in its portrayal of reality, one must "read" art hermeneutically. In other words, for art to release the truth it contains, it must be "recognised" by someone who is concerned to understand its message; it must be interpreted and its message applied in a way befitting the horizon of understanding of the interpreter.

Alasdair MacIntyre offers a useful reflection on this description. In Rembrandt's day, his portrait *The Nightwatch* was condemned as being too expressive, too far from presenting a "mirror-image" of its subjects. We know today, however, that the value of the painting lies not in its proximity to a "mirror-image", but in the way Rembrandt portrays certain features of his subjects' respective appearances that would not normally be self-evident if seen in "real life". The painted

---

[74] Heidegger, *Early Greek Thinking* (San Francisco: Harper and Row, 1975), pp. 102f. See also Warnke, *Gadamer*, pp. 57-58.

[75] Gadamer, *TM*, p. 102. On the art of writing, Gadamer states, "What is fixed in writing has detached itself from the contingency of its origin and made itself free for new relationships. Normative concepts such as the author's meaning or the original reader's understanding represent in fact only an empty space that is filled from time to time in understanding" (*TM*, p. 357).

[76] Cf. Gadamer, *TM*, p. 63. "In the experience of art there is present a fullness of meaning which belongs not only to this particular...object, but rather stands for the meaningful whole of life."

image, in other words, draws out certain features of the subject that might otherwise have remained hidden. In this way, Rembrandt draws attention to, illuminates and heightens aspects that, once disclosed in the painted form, reveal something essential about what it is he is representing. Hence, as MacIntyre suggests, "Rembrandt teaches us to see in the human face what we could not—and perhaps did not want to—see before".[77]

This in Gadamer's view is the pedagogical role of the truth in art: it presents its objects in such a way that we learn something about what it represents. We also, as I mentioned, learn something about ourselves as well. This double-edged dynamic set in motion by aesthetic representation and recognition is entailed in Gadamer's "fusion of horizons" metaphor as applied to art. This is to say that, in our encounter with a work of art, we experience an expanse of our own horizon as we interact with that of the artist's horizon, which in turn moves us toward new and increasingly relevant insights into the object portrayed, and into ourselves in relation to that object. This "fusion" yields a real enhancement of understanding not only of what is portrayed, but of ourselves and our world as seen in and through the experience of art.

The experience of art is in this way a form of knowledge. Its epistemic yield is a direct result of the internal dynamics of the hermeneutical experience of "fusion" that occurs whenever we encounter art and open ourselves to what it has to say. As we shall see, *mutatis mutandis*, this fusional dynamic lies close to the heart of Newman's theory of knowledge and especially of its development.

---

[77] Alasdair MacIntyre, "Contexts of Interpretation: Reflections on Hans-Georg Gadamer's *Truth and Method*", Boston University Journal, 27 (1976): pp. 41-46.

INTRODUCING GADAMER:

Gadamer and the Question of Relativism

In my room, the world is beyond my understanding.
But when I walk I see that it consists of
three or four hills and a cloud.

Wallace Stevens, "Of the Surface of Things"

In recent years, certain critics have attempted to show us the limits of our ability to make claims to knowledge and truth. Following on the famed Nietzschean quip, "There are no facts, only interpretations", so-called "post-modernists" have argued that the will-to-interpret runs straight through every human attempt to render objective statements. For this reason, hermeneutics has either taken a reactionary bent by becoming scientifically based, with the aim being to get at "the true meaning of the text", i.e. the autonomous, originary meaning as intended by the author (Betti, Hirsch); or it has abandoned science altogether to focus instead on "the free play of the text, the endless play of signifiers devoid of decidable meaning" that reduces interpretation to a free-ranging "parody" of objective truth (Derrida, Rorty).[78]

---

[78] Cf. Gary Madison, "Beyond Seriousness and Frivolity: A Gadamerian Response to Deconstruction", in Hugh Silverman, ed., *Gadamer and Heremeutics* (London: Routledge, 1991), p. 123.

Gadamer's hermeneutical project has sought a *via media* between these two positions. In denouncing foundationalism, scientific objectivity and every other so-called "metaphysics of presence",[79] Gadamer has aligned himself with the scepticism of the deconstructionists. Yet he does so without giving up on metaphysics, epistemology and objectivity altogether. Instead, Gadamer seeks an integrative system whereby one can transcend traditional metaphysics without being forced into a position of debilitating relativism. For Gadamer there can be "no hermeneutics without the claim to knowledge or truth".[80] Deconstructionist hermeneutics, to use Derrida's own words, is an "adventurous excess of a writing that is no longer directed by any knowledge".[81] By contrast, Gadamer's work attempts to show that it is not at all necessary to abandon the notions of knowledge and truth, that it is in fact fully possible to extricate truth while keeping a healthy metaphysical scepticism in tact. Just how successful Gadamer is in this attempt is what I want now to discuss.

ART, PLAY AND TRUTH

As we have seen, it is one of Gadamer's "first principles", adopted from Aristotle and Heidegger, that understanding is preeminently a practical thing.[82] Understanding is embedded in life, in relationships and experiences, in "the totality of human existence". The kind of

---

[79] Cf. Weinsheimer, *Gadamer's Hermeneutics*, pp. 249-50. "From Plato to Hegel, truth consists in the complete revelation of the thing, its full presence to an infinite mind...For Gadamer, by contrast, dialectic takes place not in the wordless realm of the Logos but instead in spoken language, not in the opposition of statement and counterstatement but in the exchanges of conversation and dialogue, in question and answer rather than assertion" (p. 250).

[80] Richard Bernstein, *Philosophical Profiles* (Philadelphia: University of Philadelphia Press, 1986), p. 61. Bernstein accurately describes the "playfulness" of a hermeneutics without truth as "negativity, deconstruction, suspicion, unmasking. Satire, ridicule, jokes and punning become the rhetorical devices for undermining 'puritanical seriousness'. This *espirit* pervades the writings of Rorty, Feyerabend and Derrida" (p. 59).

[81] Jacques Derrida, *Dissemination*, trans. B Johnson (Chicago: University of Chicago Press, 1981), p. 54.

[82] Cf. Warnke, *Gadamer*, pp. 40-48.

knowledge then that derives from either aesthetic, historical or textual understanding—for Gadamer they all share the same hermeneutical structure—is never going to be found in a pure, objective, unprejudiced state.[83] Understanding, rather, is a "shared experience" based upon the historically emergent horizon that both the interpreter and the thing interpreted hold in common.

Gadamer demonstrates this in two ways. First, he compares the structure of aesthetic experience to the playing of a game.[84] In game playing, as in aesthetic experience, we are transported out of ordinary existence and into another reality. In each we are caught up in the movement of the activity—with art it is sensual, and with game-playing it is physical—and thus lose a sense of ourselves, of our boundaries and ordinary perceptions: this is the source of the recreative effectiveness of both art and play. What allows entry into this ecstasis is, in both cases, a submission to authority—in the case of a game to its "rules", and in art to the rules and limits of its particular form of mimesis. Both acts, game-playing and art-viewing, are dependent upon a recognition of the "bindingness" of this authority, and a willingness to abide by it. Neither can a game be played nor art be understood without this act of willing submission.[85]

And yet there is a tension here. The rules of a game cannot wield any sort of intrinsic power that demands submission. They require for their existence willing players who freely abide by them, and who are thus free to alter them as needs arise. Which is to say the game itself does not exist without players willing to submit to and play by its rules; and yet it is part and parcel of game-playing that the players in their playing can decide to change the rules as needed. So on the one hand, in playing a game, players bring that game into existence in the

---

[83] It should be clear in what follows that Gadamer is dealing primarily with a conception of knowledge different in kind from a straightforward, propositional knowledge of facts, though nowhere in the *Truth and Method* is any such distinction made.

[84] Gadamer, *TM*, pp. 91-119.

[85] What we see in the dynamic of game-playing is the "primacy of the play over the consciousness of the players...The subject of the game is not the player; rather the players are merely the way the play comes into presentation". Cited in Gadamer, *TM*, p. 92.

sense that their actions and responses represent its rules. On the other hand, games that are represented in the actions and concerns of players are thus subject to change. A game, in other words, both determines the actions of its players, and is nothing other than the sum of those actions themselves in the moment of play.[86]

This same tension exists in art as well, especially in the performance arts. Actors have the same relationship to a play and its script as players have to a game and its rules. Yet this tension is in no sense counter-productive. Because no game is played nor drama performed in the same way twice, there is *development*. The rules of the game, the structure of dramatic scripts, are interpreted by the players, by the performers, in light of their own self-understandings; these self-understandings are themselves, of course, always in flux. Each repetition of the game, each dramatic performance, therefore, highlights new aspects of the original.[87] In this way art, like the way a game is played, goes beyond the limits of original intent. New dimensions of meaning are added at every turn, new challenges are presented to view oneself and the world differently.[88]

Gadamer is not unaware that this comparison of art with game-playing issues in the charge of relativism. If every new performance yields a new meaning, if every new viewing of an artwork renders free a new aspect of the object portrayed, then all we are left with is a never-ending production of "meanings", and not *the* meaning of a thing. And this Gadamer wants to avoid. He is too concerned to show that art represents *truth* and evokes a *truth-response*, and not

---

[86] Cf. Roy Howard, *The Three Faces of Hermeneutics* (Berkeley: University of California Press, 1982), p. 143, for a similar discussion about the nature of game-playing.

[87] This rule of interpretation holds true for the spectator or critic as well. Johnson's *Macbeth* is clearly different from Coleridge's, for example. This variety, however, "does not involve merely a...subjective variety of conceptions, but instead the possibilities of what the work itself can be, as it interprets itself in the variety of its aspect" [Gadamer, *TM*, p. 106].

[88] John MacQuarrie significantly thinks this particular aspect of Gadamer's thought to be especially appropriate to understanding the way Christology has developed in its various stages from Christ-event to Gospel to Christological reflection. In each case of expansion, it is a "recognition of the essence" of the original event. Cf. John MacQuarrie, *Jesus Christ in Modern Thought* (London: SCM Press, 1990) p. 15.

merely an artist's creativity or an audience's subjective interpretation.

Thus Gadamer proceeds to outline his theory of mimesis as I discussed above. With a reinterpreted mimesis theory, Gadamer shows that art is a real learning experience; that following the form of Hegelian dialectic, and backed by a metaphysics of "play", we can be confident that the new insights we achieve into what art portrays are rightly labelled as "truth". It serves my purposes to offer a summary of this account, and I want to do so in the following way:

a) Art, like game-playing, exerts a "normative authority" over the viewer and in doing so,

b) it makes a "binding" claim on the viewer.

c) This claim is a "truth-claim" from which one can gain a new view of oneself and the world. Hermeneutical aesthetics, therefore, is

d) primarily about understanding the truth-claims of artists and,

e) is potentially life-changing. But it is only so when,

f) one willingly submits to those truth-claims, and subsequently comes to understand what they mean for oneself, applying that understanding in a personally appropriate way.

This outline however raises more questions than it answers. If as Gadamer asserts the meaning of art is determined by the understanding of the viewer, can any definitive meaning ever be achieved? If abstracting the knowledge in art requires both a recognition of and a submission to its "normative authority", how do we avoid simply mimicking what the artist says? How can we be sure what the artist says is right? Why should we learn from Rembrandt or Monet and not some lesser known's work? Or is all artistic mimesis equally truthful? If not, how can we determine which is true mimesis and which false?

Gadamer addresses these issues with a three-fold answer that yields, important for our purposes, a clearer definition of what he means by "truth in art". First, he writes that understanding art is

primarily a matter of recognising that it is making a claim to *know*
something about the nature of human life and the world in which we
live. Any art form is an expression of this claim to knowledge.[89] And
until I willingly submit myself to this fact, the fact of its *claim* to be
epistemic, I will never be open to experiencing that claim, and
therefore to the possibility of understanding the "truth" the artwork
intends to convey.

Second, I cannot understand art if it is not relevant to my life.[90]
Just as I cannot understand a text written in a language I do not
know, neither can I understand art unless it speaks in my "language".
Its truth-claim, in other words, must always be understood from the
horizon of my own personal concerns, experiences, convictions, etc.
The significance of art is specific to each individual. The differences in
the production of a play, for example, are not unessential to its
meaning, but rather have a significance dependent upon each
reader's, director's or viewer's apprehension of the play's "truth".
Gadamer therefore concludes:

> Interpretation is probably in a certain sense re-creation. This
> re-creation, however, does not follow a preceding creative act;
> it rather follows the figure of the created work that each person
> has to bring to representation in accordance with the meaning
> he finds in it.[91]

And third, it follows from the first two points that the truth-claims
made by art are *not* universal. "The concept of a claim", writes

---

[89] Even the more extreme forms of abstract art, Gadamer writes, though they have led to the
"total elimination of any reference to an external object", still do not negate our ability to learn
something about reality from them. Only now, "we must make an active contribution of our
own...to make an effort to synthesize". Cf. Gadamer, *RB*, pp. 8-10.

[90] Up to the eighteenth century, Gadamer explains, art represented the integration of the
human community, political society, and the Church. With the advent of historicism, however,
this integration ceased to exist. Formerly when artists were linked into one aspect of this three-
fold community, representation justified itself by serving as a cohesive force. Today, with
pluralism and the breakdown of more unitary modes of community, the artist's task is to create
for herself a community "as is appropriate to [her] pluralistic situation". It is only in this
personal sense that art becomes relevant as a community-creating apparatus. Cf. *RB*, p. 7.

[91] Gadamer, *TM*, p. 107; cf. Georgia Warnke, *Gadamer*, pp. 65-67.

Gadamer, "...contains the idea that it is not itself a fixed demand".[92]
The content works of art impose upon their audience therefore cannot
be specified outside of the particular situations in which the works are
seen. They have, to use E D Hirsch's phrase, no "determinate
meaning".[93] Indeed a claim, Gadamer continues, denotes merely the
ground that enables the fulfilment of art's pedagogical function. A
truth-*claim* issued by an art-work merely provides the occasion for
my understanding it, and is not directly responsible for its content.
Art's truth-*content*, on the other hand, is determined by my
participating understandingly in the art-work's horizon; by what
"happens" at the level of the "fusion of horizons". Truth-content thus
is dependent on the degree of openness I bring to the work, my level of
perceptiveness, amount of previous experiences enabling me to share
in its language, and so on. In other words, fusion occurs in the
mediation of an object's meaning with the horizon of one's own
experiences. Understanding is effected by this fusion. The kind of
knowledge that is available in art, therefore, and by extension in all
the *Geisteswissenschaften*, is always to be found in the form of this
fusion. Which is to say that aesthetic truth, the truth found in art, is
always mediated, always subjectively apprehended and interpreted,
always defined and appropriated relative to human finitude.

Obviously, this still leaves us squarely within the bounds of
relativism, and indeed of the very subjectivity Gadamer had criticised
in Kant. Does Gadamer simply identify the truth in an aesthetic object
with what the viewer happens to find in it? Is one's personal
interpretation entirely arbitrary? If not, what then are to be our
criteria of judgment? These questions have been addressed by modern
hermeneuticians with a considerably greater degree of pessimism
than Gadamer seems to possess. They draw the conclusion that in
any form of interpretative understanding there is "an inexpungeable
subjective factor" involved, and indeed an "element of sheer

---

[92] Gadamer, *TM*, p. 112.
[93] Cited in Warnke, *Gadamer*, p. 67.

arbitrariness" (A. Danto).[94] One such scholar, Harold Bloom, has determined that all interpretation is *misinterpretation* and hence "utterly subjective".[95]

To resort to a re-worked theory of mimesis is clearly not enough. Furthermore, when the theory is examined more closely it reveals a serious contradiction: if mimesis is an *education* into what art says to us in the form of truth-claims, how then is it also a *participation*, as we saw in the comparison with game-playing, on the part of the viewing subject? In other words, how can one both submit to art's "normative authority", and at the same time have the freedom, as have the players of a game with respect to its rules, to interpret in a *personal* way what art presents? Does not my interpretative stance assume a certain detachment from authoritative norms, a certain critical distance?

PREJUDICE AND TRADITION

It seems, therefore, that Gadamer has left us in the uncomfortable predicament of choosing between a passive authoritarianism on the one hand, or a completely subjective relativism on the other. And if the two are combined, if the truth in art is merely a truth-for-us to which we yet submit as authoritative, what then is to stop art from being misappropriated for opportunistic means? What is to prevent art from degenerating into propaganda, as it did in Nazi Germany (for one among many examples)?

Indeed it could, and if one were to draw this conclusion from Gadamer's theory of mimesis, it would not be unrepresentative; but it would certainly be out of step with the kind of interpretation Gadamer himself envisaged. In his autobiographical *Philosophical*

[94] Arthur Danto, *Analytical Philosophy of History* (Cambridge: Cambridge University Press, 1968), p. 142.
[95] Harold Bloom, *The Anxiety of Influence: A Theory of Poetry* (Oxford: Oxford University Press, 1973), p. 95.

Investigations, Gadamer insists that his theory has a purely academic intention, and he expresses the hope that at least some of his critics would understand it that way.[96] Yet the central question remains: has a hermeneutical aesthetics the power to distinguish between historical situatedness and *distortion*?

This question becomes even more embroiled in controversy the further I proceed down the list of Gadamer's main themes. So far I have been led to conclude that truth in general, and aesthetic truth in particular, is situational, projectional, interpretative and (so it follows) subject-dependent; that it exists always in complex form as a "fusion" of very varied horizons. And because it is subject-dependent, and thus inextricably linked to contextual frames of time and place, it is mutable. How then, I am now asking, are we ever to arrive at trustworthy clues for weeding out what is true only for me from what is true *for all*—or at least *most*? Gadamer attempts to answer this question (though he only further complicates it), and his answer takes us straight to the source of so much anti-Gadamerian criticism. It is Gadamer's firm but controversial opinion that the *questio juris* can best be solved by rehabilitating the notions of "prejudice" and "tradition".

Since the Enlightenment, the term "prejudice" has for the most part been understood in a pejorative sense. Following on the Cartesian model of radical doubt, "prejudice" has been seen as a kind of distorting bias that tends toward easy, unverified judgments, and that must be extricated in order to make room for certain knowledge. But this view is hardly justified, says Gadamer. It is what Gadamer calls a "prejudice against prejudice".[97] For if one studies the Latin etymology of the word, *praejudicium*, which both English and German [*Vorurteil*] preserve, one sees that it is more or less value-neutral; that it embodies cognitive-reflective processes that may or may not be skewed to disadvantage. "Actually prejudice means a

---

[96] Gadamer, *PA*, p. 99.
[97] Gadamer, *TM*, p. 240.

judgment that is given before all the elements that determine a
situation have been finally examined";[98] i.e. it is a judgment like any
other, for what judgment can honestly say that it rests on a *totality* of
evidence and a *finality* of examination? In ancient Roman courts, a
praejudicata opinio was what the judge rendered before the
litigational process began; it offered the proceedings a starting-point
in the dialogue that would eventually lead to either conviction or
acquittal. The *praejudicum* could always be overturned, but the
onus probandi rested on the party that opposed it. So too
"prejudice": it is a trial judgment or hypothesis, made perhaps
without much deliberation, but still essential as fodder for all future
deliberations.

Gadamer wants to make the strong claim that all our knowing
activity is tainted by prejudice, whether for good or for ill. His
argument runs as follows: we have seen that, according to Gadamer,
there is a deep ontological connection between human existence and
the world that surrounds it—what I have called, following
Heidegger, the "temporal-regionality of *Dasein*". This situatedness,
in turn, comprises each individual's self-understanding in a way that
is unique to him or her. Self-understanding is constituted, on the one
hand, by our particular time and place in history; and on the other
hand, by the language we speak and do our thinking in. As so
constituted, it is ever expanding as it continuously assimilates our
experiences of "other" forms of self-understanding in and through
our daily involvements with the world around us.

This self-understanding, Gadamer now wants to assert, is the
substance of our prejudices. We can no more root them out than deny
our very existence. Consciousness is thus not a *tabula rasa* we can
wipe clean at will, but is always already filled with active
determinants of meaning that, whenever we try to understand
something, project themselves *qua* "pre-judgments" onto our
perceptions of the thing. This is not, Gadamer stresses repeatedly, a

[98] Gadamer, *TM*, p. 255.

situation that can be overcome; it is written into the very fabric of being human.

Gadamer links his analysis of "prejudice" to his argument for the epistemic value of "tradition" [*Überlieferung*]. Prejudices invade our self-understanding through the traditions that surround us, and in which we are sub-consciously immersed. In the form of our pre-judgments, traditions influence our thinking and interpretations whether or not we will them to. We cannot approach Shakespeare, for example, in a tradition-less vacuum, for our understanding of Shakespeare is always already dependent upon how he has been understood over the past four centuries. Even if we wished to decontruct the Shakespearean canon, we could only do so within the same interpretative structures the tradition has established as normative for Shakespeare studies. We may wish to go beyond our own traditions in order to give Shakespeare a Hindu spin, say, or a pan-African gloss. But these non-Western horizons would then only be merging with the rule of orthodox interpretations we have long since learned. In other words, we can only extend, not extinguish, the "effect" our own traditions exert upon us.[99]

But does any of this bring us any nearer a solution to the problem of Gadamer and relativism? Obviously not. For cannot the same tradition be interpreted by different people in different ways? And if so, how do we judge between them? While not addressing these questions directly, Gadamer does attempt to broaden his explanatory hypothesis with three practical principles: anticipation, application and conversation.

"Anticipation" [*Vorgriff*] is a holdover from Gadamer's appropriation of Gestalt psychology as he brings it to bear on the exegetical dynamic of the so-called "hermeneutical circle". The

---

[99] Gadamer, *TM*, p. 268. Gadamer describes these effects of tradition as the principle of "effective-history", *Wirkungsgeschichte*, or the actual operation of history on the process of understanding itself. The interpreter, he insists, cannot escape the impact of effective-history. This is what historical objectivism overlooks. As Gadamer remarks, "The power of effective-history does not depend on its being recognized".

principle of anticipation determines that prejudices can be sorted out in terms of their appropriateness not *before* they are used in the act of interpretation, in order then to be discarded altogether, but only *in* the process of interpretation itself. This thesis follows on what we have seen Gadamer do with the Aristotelian doctrine of *phronesis*, that understanding is best when it takes place in the practical, experiential working out of questions and their solutions. Here in his hermeneutical discussion, he relates it to the part-whole method of exegesis most often associated with the interpretation theories of Friedrich Schleiermacher and Wilhelm Dilthey: i.e. the so-called "hermeneutical circle".

In employing the hermeneutical circle, the interpreter begins by assuming the text has something meaningful to convey. Without this initial assumption, the interpreter will lack, in the words of Michael Polanyi, the essential "obligation toward the truth", the willingness to "submit to reality" that guides interpretation toward new discoveries.[100] Next, by projecting understanding onto the text, the interpreter "anticipates" the meaning of the text "as a whole" *before* arriving at the whole itself.[101] But far from being held to rigorously, this anticipation is subject to continual revision as more parts of the whole come into view. The goal, of course, is to find for all the parts some form of coherent integration. Once this integration is achieved, the circle is closed and the whole can be said to be understood in terms of itself, i.e. without remainder, *and* without antecedent prejudices. By this method, ideally, if one does not *begin* in an unprejudiced state, at least one *ends* there.

As we have seen, the conception of the hermeneutic circle is based both on the insight that one must "anticipate" or "project" meaning in order to understand a thing, and on the claim that this initial projection can be corrected as one's understanding deepens. Gadamer points out that the thing to be understood forms a unity, an

---

[100] Michael Polanyi, *Personal Knowledge* (Chicago: University Press, 1958), p. 63.
[101] Gadamer, *TM*, pp. 262-64.

internally consistent whole, and that one can use this regulative ideal of unity, this "prejudice toward completion" [*Vorurteil der Vollkommenheit*], to assess the adequacy of one's interpretations of its various parts.[102] It is this prejudice toward internal consistency that provides the standard for keeping, revising or discarding interpretative pre-judgments about the thing.   Aesthetic and hermeneutic efforts are thus to be aimed at finding interpretations that both make sense out of the individual parts, and integrate them into a coherent whole.

There are problems with this scheme, however.   For if one begins with an "anticipation of the whole", and views the understanding of the parts in light of that anticipation, it is not clear how these parts, so understood, can ever lead one to revise one's understanding of the whole.   Conversely, if one projects a meaning of the whole on the basis of an interpretation of the way in which individual parts cohere, how can the understanding of the whole, so projected, lead one to change one's understanding of the parts?   The hermeneutical circle, it seems, is just that—a self-enclosed circle—and not a means by which to gain critical distance.

Gadamer was not unaware of this *lapsus*.   "Here the question arises...how is one supposed to find his way out of the boundaries of his own fore-meanings?"[103]   This query leads him to search for and formulate a more practical way to ascertain the validity of prejudice and tradition: the principle of "application".

Gadamer's principle of "application" [*Anwendung*][104] begins with the question, How does hermeneutics avoid becoming merely an apology for the tradition?   In reply, Gadamer turns once again to Aristotle.   In his general treatment of ethics, Aristotle conceives of

---

[102] Deconstructionist critics have recently disputed this methodological commitment to a text's unity by drawing attention to tensions and contradictions which all texts seem to possess. Such inconsistencies include the gap between intention and meaning, content and rhetoric, and the like. See, for example, Paul de Man, *Blindness and Insight: Essays on the Rhetoric of Contemporary Criticism* (Oxford: Oxford University Press, 1971).

[103] Gadamer, *TM*, pp. 84-85.

[104] Cf. Gadamer, *TM*, pp. 29f, 274f, 281f, 294-303.

ethical knowledge as the ability to apply theoretical principles to real-life situations. Gadamer wants to find a contemporary example of this sort of *phronetic* reasoning, and he does so in the field of legal hermeneutics. He argues that the interpretation of laws, far from constituting an exceptional problem in hermeneutics, works from the same sort of situation-based reasoning Aristotle had espoused for concrete decision-making. It also provides a valid paradigm for the way ideas from past (legal) traditions can be applied judiciously to present situations. For legal counsellors are, in fact, hermeneuts; to do their job properly, they must delve deeply into the meaning of historical laws and legal texts, in order then to formulate effective arguments for current cases. It is the intent of their investigative-interpretative work to find legitimate, fitting forms of legal precedent; i.e. to apply past judgments to present questions.

Such applicative understanding, Gadamer goes on to add, yields a *development* of the legal tradition; for it entails seeing the legal tradition "at every moment, in every particular situation, in a new and different way".[105] A legal decision made in 1910, for example, may have had limited currency back when it was made; but now, in light of new particulars gathering themselves around the same or similar problem, it takes on new meaning. Its significance as a judgment *then* becomes more when it is applied *now*. Hence application is an essential ingredient in development, and thus in expanding the range of present horizons of understanding. It represents the more dynamic element in the "fusion of horizons": through their application, interpretations are judged to be fit or unfit relative to the particular situation at hand.

This same principle holds true for aesthetic understanding, notes Gadamer. The truth contained in and conveyed by a work of art must be such that it can be applied to the interpreter's concrete situation if it is to be understood at all. For aesthetic truth to "happen", it must be a truth that makes sense for and to the apprehending subject. It must be

---

[105] Gadamer, *TM*, p. 275; cf. pp. 290-305.

concretised for it to have any reality; just as for legal interpretation it is the concrete situation that determines the normative interpretation of general legislative principles. This is the epistemological flip-side of Gadamer's argument, following a tradition laid down by Kierkegaard and Nietzsche, and given systematic voice by Heidegger: namely, that the fullness of self-understanding is never achieved apiorily through conceptual abstraction, but is something that is only realised through engagement with concrete life-experiences and the interpretative struggle to understand them. "The self that we are does not possess itself", writes Gadamer; "one could say that it 'happens'".[106] Just as self-understanding obtains its reality through concretion, so too does the truth of art attain to its truth through concrete application.

But application does not take place in empty spaces; there must be a degree of self-interest involved for it to go forward at all. Hence Gadamer's analysis of self-understanding shows that it always already has in place a variety of pre-understandings of what is to be applied, certain "first principles" that govern the orientational mode of every application. Tradition passes on these principles, and we approach the thing to be understood with these principles in mind whether or not we acknowledge them. In this way the tradition, working through self-understanding, acts as a "guiding image" orienting all forms of interpretative understanding. As Gadamer writes, "In the last analysis, *all* understanding is self-understanding".[107]

And yet tradition is not a dogmatic voice imposing its heuristic structures from some timeless, omnipotent source. Tradition is a human effect, conditioned by history, and as such is always open toward the future. We cannot change past traditions, nor their influence as starting points in the continual dialogue of human understanding. But because understanding *is* such a dialogue, we

---

[106] Gadamer, *PH*, p. 55.
[107] Gadamer, *PH*, p. 55.

are ever reflecting back into the tradition our present interpretation and thus modifying it, sometimes beyond recognition. Though providing a necessary interpretative framework for every attempt at understanding, tradition is itself transformed in accordance with the concrete circumstances of the interpretation-event itself. As Georgia Warnke explains:

> The text handed down to us is a fusion of previous opinions about it, a harmony of voices, as Gadamer often puts it, to which we add our own. But this means that the object of hermeneutic understanding is already a fusion of the interpretations of a tradition and our encounter with it is an encounter with the tradition....[in such a way that] the views of a tradition are not simply adopted but modified in accordance with changed historical circumstances.[108]

This leaves us, however, with a peculiar oscillation in Gadamer's treatment of tradition. On the one hand, we are indebted to tradition for all our interpretations, however non-traditional they may be; while on the other hand, present circumstances possess the power to alter the traditional framework of interpretation in order to meet changing standards of evaluation. Has Gadamer thus left us suspended between a conservative traditionalism on the one hand, and the potential for an indiscriminate opportunism on the other? Not necessarily. He is sensitive to this critique and thus proposes to resolve the tension with his third hermeneutical principle, that of "conversation".[109]

For Gadamer, "conversation" [Gespräch] is of the essence of all authentic human understanding. But no genuine conversation can take place if each conversant pridefully expounds his or her own views, and fails to listen to what the others have to say. Hence, true conversation must begin with a confession of loyalty to the Socratic

---

[108] Georgia Warnke, *Gadamer*, pp. 90-92. See also Joel Weinsheimer, *Gadamer's Hermeneutics*, pp. 205f.
[109] Cf. Gadamer, *TM*, pp. 163, 165, 330f, 344f, 487f.

docta ignorantia: we are to acknowledge our "finitude"; to admit that we do not know everything; that other, more expansive horizons have much to teach us. With this attitude in place, we are then "open" to looking for the truth in what "the other" has to say.

The "other" need not be another person. The hermeneutical event of truth takes place whenever we want to understand something; and this understanding, Gadamer is now saying, is always already *conversational*. Whether we read a book, view a painting or listen to a symphony; whether we stare sublimely into the night sky, our lover's eyes or the bottom of a deep well; whether we laugh, cry or sing in the face of death, we are in each case engaged in a "conversation" with "the other". And as a good *Gesprächpartner*, we assume this "other" has something significant to say; that if we "listen" with enough attention, we will hear "it" speak to us of things we can call "true". In this sense, conversation is a hermeneutical act of self-improvement; when we are "caught up" in a conversation, as when we are "caught up" in game-playing, we come out in the end being *more*. Conversation is the act of striving to break out of our limited horizons in order to enwrap them around ones that are larger.

Gadamer claims that the aim of every conversation is to come to some kind of "agreement" [*Übereinstimmung*] with what the "other" is saying. And if this can be achieved, we will have transcended our own limited horizons and attained a "new view" of the subject. Even if our "conversation" degenerates into debate and we find nothing on which we can agree, we will still have accomplished something: for we will have re-defined the borders of our own horizons by clarifying them *over against* "the other", thus extending the range of our self-interpretative vocabularies.

Socratic-Hegelian dialectic is the prototype for this principle of "conversation"; and the "fusion of horizons", as we have seen, is the metaphor used to describe how it operates. The "integration" that results from such a fusion determines that the content of the subject-matter, regardless of whether an agreement is reached between the two "conversation partners", is always in some way taken up by the one trying to understand it, always makes its way into consciousness and transforms it. We may not agree with Wordsworth's romantic cosmology, for example, yet in our engagement with his poetry we are forced to put our own cosmological views in question, and in the questioning, perhaps, to alter them.[110]

Gadamer's point here is that a reasoned account of any aspect of a tradition involves some degree of appropriating it and integrating it into our own understanding of the subject-matter. We cannot understand what we do not converse with, and we cannot enter into real conversation if we do not entertain the possibility that "the other" may just be speaking the truth. For only in doing so are we able to discern strands of agreement and disagreement, and use these to weave into our own horizons of understanding more universal perspectives. In short, Gadamer's point is a Hegelian one: coming to understand "the other" involves taking what it says seriously, reflecting upon it in light of our own understanding, always with a view toward both its valid, fitting insights and its mistaken opinions with regard to the subject matter in question. In the fusion that results, the truth of one's own position and that of the object are both preserved in a new stage of the tradition; and at the same time, they are cancelled as independently-existing opinions that may or may not have been valid in their own right.[111]

Still questions arise: Is this not a more subtle form perhaps of the very traditionalism Gadamer is so obviously at pains to avoid? For do not most conversations end up with one person's point of view dominating? Consider the Platonic dialogues: did not Socrates

---

[110] Hirsch points to conflicting interpretations of Wordsworth's "A Slumber Did my Spirit Seal" as an example of the predicament to which the prejudiced character of textual interpretation leads. Different initial assumptions have led to competing views on the meaning of the poem's final lines. Each competing view, however, is equally rooted in traditions of Wordsworth scholarship. The question that arises then is whether it is possible to choose between them. In E. D. Hirsch, *Validity in Interpretation* (New Haven: Yale University Press, 1967) pp. 227f.

[111] Gadamer references this methodology with what he calls the "priority of the question". A question places given subject-matter within a particular perspective or horizon. Moreover, it is in the process of to-and-fro of question and answer that fresh insights may be said to arise. Truths thus "emerge" from the whole dialectical process of interrogation. Cf. *TM*, p. 331.

usually win the day in the end? Thus if we are to avoid this seemingly inevitable predicament, and assuming that a "fusion of horizons" is the achievement of some sort of *consensus* of opinion, would we not be forced each time into an *acquiescence*, rather than a genuine *synthesis* of views?

Although these questions point to genuine abysses in Gadamer's project, I do not believe his project *as a whole* allows for any of them to be asked without qualification. While Gadamer clearly wants to portray a hermeneutical philosophy that guards the safe passage of certain traditional ideas into modern frameworks of understanding— that the Greco-Roman classics are superior to modern writings; that the human sciences are more important for moral education than the natural, etc.— it is equally clear in his writings that we also must be critically selective. In an important statement, Gadamer writes, "Every encounter with tradition...involves the experience of the tension between the text and the present".[112] But the latter pole of this tension seems often to miss mention. Gadamer speaks of tradition in much the same way he treats of good art: its authority that we take to be normative "enchants" us before we can ever hope to assess that claim.[113]

But again, it bears repeating that Gadamer's hermeneutical analysis of the conditions of understanding generally does *not* support such a strong traditionalism. We always agree with the tradition in the sense that we are inextricably a part of it, and therefore to greater or lesser degrees are oriented by it. But it is an indefeasible demand of every hermeneutical encounter that there be a reversal of direction; that in our engagement with the tradition we also modify it as we seek to agree *conversationally* upon the truth of the subject-matter with which both we and it are concerned. Which is to say, we not only assess certain traditional values in light of other values we inherit from the very same traditions, we also sometimes

---

[112] Gadamer, *TM.*, p. 273.
[113] Cf. Warnke on this point, in *Gadamer*, pp. 105-06.

alter those values altogether with insights garnered from our own, post-traditional—and changed—historico-linguistic circumstances. It is Gadamer's consistent appeal that we need not always agree with our inherited traditions in the substantive sense, but only in the sense that their views are integral with our own, whether we agree with them or not. As we shall see, this is a view that holds much in common with Newman's own theory of how Christian traditions both inform, and are transformed by, the people who commit themselves to them.

PART ONE:

Newman's Philosophical Genealogy

> *A foolish consistency is the hobgoblin of little minds,*
> *adored by little statesmen*
> *and philosophers*
> *and divines.*
>
> Ralph Waldo Emerson, "Self-Reliance"

Having completed now my lengthy discursis into Gadamer's thought, it is time to return to Newman, and to the principle aim of this book: namely, to represent and evaluate Newman's theory of religious knowledge. Newman is rarely known as a philosopher, however; and so it seems appropriate to investigate the extent to which he had familiarised himself with the philosophical issues of his day, and from which sources he may have gathered his philosophical ideas.[114]

There are four main schools of philosophy to which Newman was particularly indebted throughout his life. These are, in no particular order, Aristotle and Aristotelianism, the probability and typology theories of Joseph Butler's *Analogy of Religion*, the Platonism of the Alexandrian Fathers and the empiricism of John Locke. There are in

---

[114] To my knowledge, with the possible exception of Edward Sillem's helpful but somewhat superficial work in his introudction to *PN*, no one has made any lengthy study of Newman's philosophical sources.

addition several "minor" sources, including the psychological theories
of Abraham Tucker and Joshua Reynolds, the accounts of reason in
Bacon and Newton, the so-called Oriel "Noetics" (perhaps *not* such
a "minor source"), Berkeley, Hume, the Scottish Common Sense
School, J. S. Mill, and to a much lesser extent, German Idealism.[115]

To be exhaustive in this task would be to hearken back to
Newman's earliest days at Oxford when he was an undergraduate
commoner at Trinity. It was this Oxford, the Oxford of his passionate
youth and burgeoning professional and spiritual lives that Newman
loved so much, and that stamped its permanent impression upon his
mind. But I must be brief, and so will exclude this important
background material, as well as all but the briefest of comment on the
above listed "minor" sources. Instead, I want to give a summary of
Newman's involvement with the four "main" schools of thought, and
from which he culled the bulk of his personal philosophy, before
closing with a brief discussion on the reasons for his first ignoring,
then abandoning altogether the German tradition.

ARISTOTLE

The first formative influence that helped shape the foundations of
Newman's philosophy, and as ought to be clear from the foregoing is
his most immediate philosophical connection to Gadamer, was his
early study of Aristotle. It is noteworthy that Newman left Aristotle
out altogether in the account of his intellectual life, the *Apologia*.
This can perhaps best be explained by saying that the *Apologia* was
written merely as an apology for his *religious* life and changing
convictions, and as such was never intended to be an account for his
thought-life as a whole. But in turning to his larger corpus of
writings, one finds many tributes to Aristotle among them.

While an undergraduate at Trinity College, Oxford, Newman

---

[115] Cf. Newman, *PN*, vol. 1, pp. 203-220.

made an intensive study of Aristotle's *Rhetoric, Poetics* and *Nicomachean Ethics*, all three of which he had to prepare for his commoner's Greek exams.[116] Important for my purposes is to note Edward Sillem's comment that from these works Newman derived his "life-long reflections on *experimental* knowledge", which led in later years, as I will show below, to his distinctive doctrine of the "illative sense".[117]

In 1821, at the age of twenty, Newman published his first article, in the *Christian Observer*, and entitled, "On the Analogous Nature of the Difficulties in Mathematics and those of Religion". From its distinctive Aristotelian character, one can readily see the degree to which his Schools preparation had influenced him. Seven years later, Newman was to publish a more substantive essay entitled "Poetry with Reference to Aristotle's *Poetics*" in the *London Review*.[118] This latter article, in fact, offers Newman's youthful "speculations" into the nature of poetry in general, and Greek tragedy in particular, with Aristotle used only as a springboard into a much broader range of classical literature. It thus reveals, significantly, the direction in which he wanted to take his study of Aristotle—namely into the realm of *aesthetics*.

In the Michaelmas term of 1822, at the age of twenty-one, and by now a Junior Research Fellow at Oriel College, Oxford, Newman was enlisted by Richard Whateley (1787-1863), senior philosophy tutor at Oriel and later archbishop of Dublin, to assist him in his work on Aristotle's *Logic*. Newman worked closely with his "mentor" for four years. He perhaps learned less about Aristotle, however, than about how to cipher even the most obtuse of philosophical arguments into beautifully stylised prose—for Whately was, if anything, a

---

[116] In a trip to the Birmingham Oratory (August, 1991) I leafed through Newman's own copy of Aristotle's *Nicomachean Ethics* (1818 version) in the original language. It was well-worn, full of smudge prints, with every margin containing Newman's comments, translations, philological studies, cross-references, and the like. It was clear that he had studied the entire text thoroughly, and had returned to his marginal notes time and time again.

[117] Newman, *PN*, vol. 1, p. 151. Italics added.

[118] Cf. Ian Ker, *John Henry Newman* (Oxford: Oxford University Press, 1988), p. 31.

consummate stylist. Newman too, of course, was no slouch when it came to rhetorical flourish, and as a result of the younger Fellow's "suggested remarks and alterations",[119] Whateley in 1826 published *Elements of Logic*, his *magnum opus*. In its day, and quite surprisingly for an otherwise dull-witted philosophical treatise, it was widely read. For his efforts, Newman received a real education into the importance of combining genuine philosophical insights with literary artistry if one wished to reach a wider readership.

Newman was not an uncritical reader of Aristotle, and seems to have taken from him selectively. He had little if any contact with either the *Physics* or the *Metaphysics*, and there are no traces in his writings of the leading Aristotelian ideas of potency and act, or the "form-matter hypothesis". Newman adopted Aristotle's theory of "real knowledge", for example, while at the same time rejecting his more straightforward rationalism. It may have been, as one writer put it, that Aristotle's metaphysical system was far too "physical" for Newman's more "sacramental" sentiments.[120]

In fact, by the time he published *Arians of the Fourth Century* (1833), Newman had arrived at the opinion that Aristotelianism and the loftier sentiments of orthodoxy were more or less incompatible. He wrote vociferously against Arius and his followers, denouncing him as a typical example of how an uncritical adoption of "Aristotelian logic corrupts the theological mind". It was Newman's opinion that being skilled in the arts of sophistry and disputation is no substitute for deep piety. For this reason he approved of "a writer of the fourth century, who calls Aristotle the Bishop of the Arians".[121] Newman evidently felt better disposed toward the dialectically challenged, quoting the words of St. Ambrose (inserted also on the title page of the *Grammar of Assent*): "Non in dialectica complacuit Deo salvum facere populum suum".[122]

---

[119] Richard Whateley, *Elements of Logic* (London: Sheed and Ward, 1828), p. viii.
[120] Cf. Newman, *PN*, vol. 1, p. 158.
[121] Newman, *Arians*, p. 29.

Criticisms of Aristotle occur as well in Newman's *University Sermons*, which themselves form the thematic background to his more straightforwardly philosophical treatise, *Grammar of Assent*. In the second sermon (1830), Newman criticises Aristotle's theory of the virtuous man;[123] and in the fourth (1831), he found that in the early centuries of Christianity,

> while Faith was engaged in that exact and well-instructed devotion to Christ which no words can suitably describe, the forward Reason stepped in upon the yet unenclosed ground of doctrine, and attempted to describe there, from its own resources, an image of the Invisible.[124]

The "forward Reason" in this passage belonged to those who had strayed from orthodoxy, who had "rationalised" the Faith by their use of Aristotelian logic. In a footnote appended to a later edition, Newman cites the early theologian Epiphanius to this effect.

But Newman is a man, as I said, of polymorphous opinions, able on demand to change their shape to fit the contours of his current circumstances. It is thus not surprising to find that Newman *the Roman Catholic convert* was far more welcoming of Aristotle, and subsequently of Aristotelian-inspired theology. In his *Idea of a University* (1854), written to bolster his induction of a new Catholic University in Dublin, Newman wrote:

> While we are men, we cannot help, to a great extent, being Aristotelians, for the great master does but analyse the thoughts, feelings, views, and opinions of human kind. He has told us the meaning of our own words, and ideas, before we were born. In many subject-matters, to think correctly, is to

---

[122] Cf. Newman, *Arians*, p. 29 where the passage is quoted in a footnote, and *AVS*, p. 264. The quotation comes from Ambrose, *de Fide*, I. 5, § 42.

[123] A lengthier and somewhat more eloquent parody is given in *Idea* , VIII, § 10. "From the very accuracy and steadiness of his logical powers", writes Newman, "he is able to see what sentiments are consistent in those who hold any religious doctrine at all, and he appears to others to feel and to hold a whole circle of theological truths, which exist in his mind no otherwise than as a number of deductions".

[124] Newman, *US*, p. 65.

> think like Aristotle, and we are his disciples whether we will
> or no...[125]

Elsewhere Newman writes of the way Aquinas transfigured the status of Aristotle from "a word of offence" to "a hewer of wood and a drawer of water to the Church".[126] He ascribes to Aristotle, "the most comprehensive intellect of Antiquity"; and calls him the one who mapped out "the whole field of knowledge" upon which theology is to cast its interpretative gaze.[127]

It is impossible here to explain in full the reasons for Newman's changed attitude toward Aritstotle. His switch of denominations, coming as it did on the eve of Catholicism's sweeping Thomistic revival, certainly would have put his own more Platonic-patristic sympathies on the defensive. But I think a more adequate explanation can be found in Newman's new role as educator—he was to be Rector of the above mentioned University. Faced with the task of selling education to the Catholic public, Newman may have discovered in Aristotle a potent set of arguments for the "unity of knowledge", for the "harmony" among the various separate disciplines he was hoping to create at Dublin; a "harmony" in which each finds its place in an overall Catholic education into the virtues proper to healthy living.

More significant for my purposes, however, is Newman's use of Aristotle when dealing with explicitly epistemological problems. In the *Grammar of Assent*, Newman attributes his ideas in ethics and practical knowledge not only to the Gospels, but also to the "heathen moralists", by whom he means Cicero and Aristotle.[128] He quotes at length from the *Nichomachean Ethics* to show what use he had made of Aristotle's ideas of moral duty and, of especial importance for its connection to Gadamer, of the role of *phronesis* in building his own doctrine of the "Illative sense".[129] He states categorically that, "as to

[125] Newman, *Idea*, pp. 109-110; cf. p. 53.
[126] Newman, *Idea*, p. 470.
[127] Newman, *HS*, "Abelard", vol. 3, p. 195.
[128] Newman, *GA*, p. 334.

the intellectual position from which I have contemplated the subject [of human knowledge], Aristotle has been my master".[130]

It is thus correct to think that it was Aristotle who put Newman on to several of the main themes that were to make up his philosophy. There is no reason to hold, as does F. M. Willan, that Newman is a "pure Aristotelian", nor even that he adopted whole-heartedly an Aristotelian picture of the human mind, as had Aquinas. There are too many non-Aristotelian elements in Newman's thought for that.

JOSEPH BUTLER

Butler [1692-1752] was an Oriel graduate, a convert from Presbyterianism to Anglicanism, and later Bishop of Durham and clerk to the royal court. Both a philosopher and theologian, a moralist and naturalist, a man of mystical faith as well as public affairs, Butler appealed deeply to Newman. He had read Butler's famed *Analogy of Religion* [1736] for the first time in 1825, as he was nearing the end of his work with Whateley on the *Elements of Logic*.[131] From this reading, mediated by his exposure to Aristotelianism and Whateley's sharp, aesthetically sensitive intellect, Newman gained two leading ideas that, in his own words, "form the underlying principles of a great portion of my teaching".[132] These were the Platonic understanding of the analogy between nature and the supernatural realm, and the doctrine that "probability is the guide of life".[133]

In the *Analogy*, Butler insists on the similarity between the works of God as seen in nature, and those that are "revealed in sacred history". He considers nature a product of providential design; thus

---

[129] Newman, *GA*, pp. 276-81. "Such is Aristotle's doctrine", says Newman, "and it is undoubtedly true".

[130] Newman, *GA*, p. 334.

[131] Newman's copy of Butler's *Analogy* is now in the main library at the Oratory. It is the first volume of his set of *The Works of Joseph Butler* (London: Longmans, 1813).

[132] Newman, *AVS*, p. 108.

[133] Newman, *AVS*, p. 21.

by studying nature one should expect to find confirmation for the revealed doctrines of Christianity. Moreover, he determines that so great is this analogical connection between nature and revelation that simply by studying nature alone, one should be able arrive at an adequate acknowledgement of God, which would then prepare the way for a more fuller indoctrination into Christian teaching. This latter thought especially appealed to Newman, the future Tractarian and defender of high-church ritualism. From it he developed what he was later to call his "sacramental principle".

> The very idea of an analogy between the separate works of God leads to the conclusion that the system which is of less importance is economically or sacramentally connected with the more momentous system, and of this conclusion the theory...is an ultimate resolution.[134]

The young Newman adopted Butler's theory wholeheartedly. It seemed to him to satisfy the particular frame of mind to which he had "felt inclined" since childhood.[135] Newman explains this mindset most fully in his essay on "Milman's View of Christianity", which ends as follows:

> All that is seen—the world, the Bible, the Church, the civil polity, and man himself—are types, and, in their degree and place, representatives and organs of an unseen world, truer and higher than themselves. The only difference between them is, that some things bear their supernatural character upon their surface, are historically creations of the supernatural system, or are perceptibly instrumental, or obviously symbolised: while others rather seem to be complete in themselves, or run counter to the unseen system which they really subserve, and thereby make demands upon our faith.[136]

---

[134] Newman, *AVS*, p. 108.
[135] Newman, *AVS*, p. 21.
[136] Newman, *EHC*, vol. 2, pp. 193. The last three pages of this essay are seminal for an understanding of Newman's "sacramental principle".

Origen's influence

Clearly this bears little substantive resemblance to the Thomistic doctrine of *analogia entis*. Butler derived his theory from middle Platonism, not Aristotle, and most notably from the middle-platonist theologian, Origen (c. 185-253), whom he cites in the introduction to *Analogy* as the inspiration behind his idea of "sacramental representation". While Thomas' teaching is the logical counterpart to the metaphysical doctrine that all contingent beings participate in Being-in-general, Butler's doctrine of analogy is more strictly a moral argument, negative in character, which attempts to prove that on acceptance of a natural order as the product of an "Intelligent Author and Governor",[137] there should be no likely reason for avoiding the higher call of virtue and the worship of God. Like Origen, Butler believed in the existence of an hierarchy of Being, each lower stage manifesting in veiled form the reality of the higher, until one comes in the final stage to the ultimate, immutable notion of Being itself. The existence of this hierarchy, "intuitively manifest" but only indirectly perceived, should enable the thoughtful person, once it is so recognised, "to live under a dutiful sense of his Maker".[138]

hierarchy of being

If his assumption that nature entails an active Creator is any indication, it seems clear that Butler did not intend his argument to appeal to the religious sceptic. He may have hoped to convince certain deists, like the disciples of Lord Shaftesbury, that their belief in a creator-God might reasonably lead them to accept the claims of Christianity. But he certainly could not have expected the treatment Newman was to give his theory of analogy. What Newman understood as Butler's more positive but implicit argument—namely, that the coincidence of two witnesses to God in the form of nature and revelation establish a line of direct correspondence between them—was extended in the *Apologia pro Vita Sua* into a more explicit argument for the existence of God from conscience:

---

[137] Joseph Butler, *Analogy of Religion Natural and Revealed* (Oxford: Clarendon Press, 1874) p. 142.

[138] Butler, *Analogy of Religion.*, p. 307.

Origenism in Newman?

And if I am asked why I believe in God, I answer that it is
because I believe in myself, for I feel it impossible to believe
also in my own existence...without believing also in the
existence of Him, who lives as a Personal, All-seeing, All-
judging Being in my conscience.[139]

From this it follows that the person who inwardly reflects upon
the mystery of personal existence, and who subsequently attains to a
"real apprehension" of the existence of God, looks out upon the world
in a new way. Material things, Newman argues, are not the norm or
standard of existence from which we derive all our knowledge;
rather, they exist "sacramentally" as a reflection of the God whose
existence we affirm, and whom we therefore come to know *inwardly*
through conscience. It is significant to my purposes to emphasise the
extension of Newman's conviction here: i.e. that what certitude about
God's existence we are able to ascertain is not of an objective nature.
It is instead subject-oriented, relative to the ebb and flow of inward
states of consciousness, and therefore difficult to explain:

The being of God...is as certain to me as the certainty of my
own existence, though when I try to put the grounds of that
certainty into logical shape I find a difficulty in doing so in
mood and figure to my satisfaction...Were it not for this voice,
speaking so clearly in my conscience and my heart, I should be
an atheist, or a pantheist, or a polytheist...[140]

The second point Newman learned from Butler, the "principle of
probability", was to play a more seminal role in laying the
groundwork for his theory of religious knowledge.[141] In the
Analogy, Butler distinguishes between "demonstrative" and
"probable" evidence and considers that "demonstrative evidence" is

---

[139] Newman, *AVS*, p. 28.

[140] Newman, *AVS.*, p. 186.

[141] Newman, *AVS*, p. 113. Newman notes that Butler's *Analogy* "led me, at least under the
teaching to which a few years later I was introduced, to the question of the logical cogency of
Faith, on which I have written so much".

only available to us in abstract thinking: in mathematics, for example, or logic. When dealing with matters of concrete realities, however—an event in history, say, or a sense impression—we can attain nothing more than "probable evidence" to show for any opinion we might hold about it. Since matters of "fact" can only be observed empirically, and the possibility of error is always present in any empirical observation, we must always preface our factual statements with a phrase like, "it is *likely* that..." or "it is *probable* that..."[142] Probable evidence of fact is thus essentially different from demonstrative evidence of induction in that "it admits of degrees, and of all variety of them, from the highest moral certainty, to the very lowest presumption".[143] Thus one can never possess absolute certainty about historical or empirical facts, including those of Christian revelation, for they are only more or less true in accordance with the probability that attends the likelihood of their occurance.

But however much this doctrine may have appealed to the young Oriel don under the liberal Whateley's tutelage, the elder Newman, Newman the Roman Catholic apologist, did not adopt this doctrine without qualification. In his *Apologia* he spoke of the "danger" of Butler's probability doctrine with its "tendency to destroy absolute certainty...resolving truth into an opinion, which it is safe to obey or to profess, but not possible to embrace with full internal assent".[144] On the contrary, argues Newman, when we look into our own experience we see that we do indeed believe wholeheartedly in a great number of statements of fact—"Great Britain is an island"[145] for one, more celebrated example—even when we cannot prove or demonstrate their truth absolutely. If probability is to be a "guide of life", it must not be incompatible with certitude. Butler's general theory, therefore, would have to be modified.

This Newman did in his *Grammar of Assent*. By distinguishing

[142] Butler, *Analogy of Religion*, Introduction, pp. 1-3.
[143] Butler, *Analogy of Religion*, p. 1; cf. Newman, *GA*, p. 59.
[144] Newman, *AVS*, 28.
[145] Newman, *GA*, p. 234.

"certitude", a state of mind, from "certainty", a quality of propositions, Newman showed that the human mind can be absolutely certain of a fact that in itself admits only of probable status. This is due to the presence in the mind of "first principles":

> It is common to call probability the guide of life. This saying, when properly explained, is true; however...it is far from true if we so hold it as to forget that without first principles there can be no conclusions at all, and that thus probability does in some sense presuppose and require the existence of truths which are certain.[146]

So Newman qualifies Butler's principle of probability with a belief in "first principles", what we would now call "basic beliefs". I want to note here in passing, and will explain later in detail, that "first principles" play a *hermeneutical* role in the knowing experience. Inasmuch as they constitute the interpretative "fore-structures" of consciousness, they provide an evaluative framework within which one may reasonably interpret probable evidence as being in greater or lesser degrees worthy of one's assent.

Newman takes the argument to a decidedly non-hermeneutical level, however, when he turns to apply it to the evidence of *religious* certitude. Here he follows his former Oriel colleague, John Keble, in declaring that without the "living power of faith and love", probabilistic arguments would have little effect. According to Newman, "faith and love" are the marks of an *objectivity* that probabilistic reasoning alone is powerless to establish:

> It is faith and love which give to probability a force which it has not in itself. Faith and love are directed toward an Object; in the vision of that Object they live; it is that Object, received in faith and love, which renders it reasonable to take probability as sufficient for internal conviction.[147]

---

[146] Newman, *GA*, p. 192.
[147] Newman, *AVS*, pp. 28-29.

It is clear then that, although he was indebted to Butler for two of his "leading ideas", Newman impresses upon them his own firmly held convictions, particularly with respect to probability as a general "guide of life". Which is not to say Butler's influence was minimal; just that he was more effective in *reinforcing* certain first principles already in place in Newman's thinking than in creating new ones. Most importantly for my purposes, Butler's *Analogy* served to open Newman's mind to the question of subjectivity and its role in the determination of epistemic certitude, however qualified that question may have been by Newman's religious sensibilities.

ALEXANDRIAN PLATONISM

Closely allied with the influence of Butler was that of the two great middle-Platonist writers, Clement [c. 150-213] and Origen [185-253], both Christian philosophers of the Alexandria school. Newman began his life-long professional interest in the Church Fathers in 1828 when he directed his energies upon the Arian controversy, though his familiarity with patristic theology had begun as early as 1816 with a reading of Joseph Milner's *Church History*. By the time he completed *Arians* in 1832, Newman had saturated himself with the thought of the two Alexandrians, finding his imagination captured by their syncretistic mix of Platonic philosophy, Stoic morality and mystical Christian piety; along with their admirable command of Greek:

> The broad philosophy of Clement and Origen carried me away; the philosophy, not the theological doctrine...Some portions of their teaching, magnificent in themselves, came like music to my inward ear, as if the response to ideas, which, with little external to encourage them, I had cherished so long.[148]

---

[148] Newman, *Arians*, p. 12.

By the time *Arians* was published, Newman's philosophical views had shifted from the liberally inclined Aristotelianism of Whateley—i.e. logical rationalism—to the mystical Platonism of the Alexandrians.[149] Prompted by his study of patristic history and all its complexity of development—its erratic twists and turns of doctrinal ideology, its promptings from political pressure and expediency, its sometimes neurotic hold on certain functional simplifications of the faith—Newman began to inquire, in more general terms, into the *historical* nature of the tradition and development of ideas. From this came his now famous theory of doctrinal development, codified in *Essay on the Development of Christian Doctrine*. Unlike the theories of "logical explication" of the Scholastics or Bossuet, which by the mid-nineteenth century had become *de rigueur* among high-church advocates, Newman's theory refused to gloss over the "untidy actualities of history and life".[150] Newman insisted, to the contrary, that the situatedness of ideas in history is something that cannot be ignored, for it is instrumental in effecting their temporal development, and hence their continuing pertinence in new historical settings. "An idea not only modifies", writes Newman in proto-Gadamerian tones, "but is *modified*, or at least *influenced*, by the state of things in which it is carried out, and is dependent in various ways on the circumstances which surround it".[151] This attention to historical context, I want to suggest, was in large part due to his study of Clement and Origen.

Newman took from Clement and Origen what he calls his "mystical" or "sacramental principle", in light of which he understood "the exterior world, physical and historical" to be "but the manifestation to our senses of realities greater than itself".[152] This has affinities with Butler's principle of analogy, of course; but now,

---

[149] For a thorough analysis of this shift, see Jan Walgrave, *Newman the Theologian* (London: Hodder and Stoughton, 1960), pp. 17-20.

[150] Ian Ker, "Foreward" to Newman's *DD*, p. xxi. All my citations from this work follow Newman's own divisions.

[151] Newman, *DD*, I. 1. 6. Italics added.

[152] Newman, *AVS*, pp. 36-37.

having had the opportunity to study at length the hellenistically influenced exegetical practices of the Alexandrians, it assumes in Newman's mind a more hermeneutical role.

Clement had postulated, and Origen perfected, a hermeneutical therapy by which the otherwise unrelated events of world history could be read as fore-shadowing, representing, even embodying the significance of those events that are deemed sacred to Christian history. Newman calls this therapy the "principle of economy". He uses the phrase in two different but related ways: to denote in a general way, first, the whole theologically interpretative process by which the original experience of the Christ event, *via* its codification in Scripture and the traditions of the early church, is lead to its eventual formulation in Christian dogma and creed; and secondly, as a positive reference to the ability of the Alexandrians, by means of the same sort of hermeneutical process, to assimilate within a broad horizon of understanding a variety of experiences and traditions lying *outside* Christian belief. To subtle minds like Origen's and Clement's—imbued, as Newman put it, with the "spirit of Hermes"— "nature was a parable; Scripture an allegory; pagan literature, philosophy, and mythology, properly understood, were but a preparation for the Gospel."[153]

As a result of his exposure to the hermeneutical tact and open-mindedness of the two Alexandrian Fathers—or perhaps it is more correct to say, as a result of his own hermeneutical sensibilities over against theirs—Newman took from his patristic studies a sense of the epistemic validity of mystery, symbol and sacrament. Even "Holy Church", says Newman, is but "a symbol of those heavenly facts which fill eternity". The church's sacraments and teachings are "but the expressions in human language of truths to which the human mind is unequal".[154] Following from this, and here very much in line with a modern theology of symbols, Newman was able to affirm that

[153] Newman, *AVS*, p. 37.
[154] Newman, *AVS*, p. 37.

does H. this critique viewing way of history?

dogmas?
at too?

verbal statements of faith—creeds, dogmas, liturgical prayers—
function for believers in the same manner as statues, candles, altars
and crucifixes; namely, as "symbols" that not only point toward, but
are in no way identical to, the objects they represent, but also in some
mysterious sense bring those objects nearer.[155] This latter emphasis
especially, once given a Gadamerian spin, opens the way for my
synthetic response to the Newman-Gadamer conversation, as I will
show in Part Four.

JOHN LOCKE

It is debatable to what extent one can attribute to Locke [1632-
1704] any decisively formative influence on Newman's philosophical
views. We know that apart from reading Hume's *Essays* at the
rather prodigious age of fourteen,[156] the first philosophical work
Newman was to study in depth was Locke's *Essay Concerning
Human Understanding*, which he read concurrently with Gibbon's
Decline and Fall of the Roman Empire during Oxford's long
vacation of 1818. Significantly, there are few notations in Newman's
personal copy of the text. What there are of markings are to be found
mainly in the fourth book of the *Essay*, and in a style that, as far as I
can make out, resembles his handwriting at about the time he wrote
the *Grammar of Assent*.[157]

While Newman admired Locke as a "manly" philosopher, in his
Grammar of Assent Locke is chosen as a key representative of the
tradition of liberal rationalism: i.e. the very tradition his polemic was
intended to disqualify. In his earlier lecture on "English Catholic
Literature", Newman makes it very clear he stands in opposition not
only to Locke but to the whole tradition of British Empiricism:

---

[155] Newman, *GA*, pp. 108-09.
[156] Newman, *AVS*, p. 2.
[157] Both the Locke text and Newman's handwritten notes for *GA* are held for private viewing at
the Birmingham Oratory.

> If we were to ask for a rapport of our philosophers, the investigation would not be so agreeable; for we have three of evil, and one of unsatisfactory repute. Locke is scarcely an honour to us in the standard of truth, grave and manly as he is; and Hobbes, Hume, and Bentham, in spite of their abilities, are simply a disgrace.[158]

Newman's sweeping dismissal is self-serving, of course. Like so much of his disputative writing, it speaks more to his ecclesiastical agenda than his professional interests as a scholar of religion. For in fact, he *did* find several points in Locke's philosophy with which he could concur. This is especially true of Locke's theory of knowledge. That each person is dependent upon personal experience for the attainment of knowledge; that as all knowledge arises from experience, it is inextricable from that experience; that there are no innate ideas apart from those that are inferred experientially—all these Newman agreed with and incorporated into his own theory of religious knowledge. Newman was at one with Locke (and, as we shall see, with Gadamer as well) in rejecting any form of *a priori* metaphysical system that puts mental concepts in the place of existent things as the basic units of reality. That this is fundamental for Newman can be seen in his praise of Hurrell Froude, another Oriel colleague, who while possessing a "keen insight into abstract truth" was nonetheless "an Englishman to the backbone in his severe adherence to the real and the concrete".[159]

Furthermore, Newman follows Locke in making *the self* the starting point of his whole philosophy, and in basing his argument for the existence of God on *self-knowledge* rather than knowledge of the external world. One should be careful not to press this connection, however, for Newman and Locke had different understandings both of the self, and of the ways in which the self is involved in the attainment of a knowledge of God. Still, it would not be an unfair

---

[158] Newman, *Idea*, p. 331 (Lecture III. § 5.2).
[159] Newman, *AVS*, p. 44.

assertion to say that, at least at the level of vocabulary, if not grammar, there is fundamental agreement between the two.

To illustrate the degree of *disagreement* between Newman and Locke, it will be necessary to quote at length two passages from the fourth book of Locke's *Essay* which, considered on their own and without any reference to their respective contexts, bear a striking resemblance to ideas typical of Newman:

> I think it is beyond question, that man has a clear idea of his own being; he knows certainly that he exists, and that he is something...If any one pretends to be so sceptical as to deny his own existence...let him for me enjoy his beloved happiness of being nothing, until hunger or some other pain convince him of the contrary. This, then...I may take for a truth...that he is *something that actually exists.*[160]

> It is plain to me we have a more certain knowledge of the existence of a God, than of anything our senses have not immediately discovered to us...We more certainly know that there is a God, than that there is anything else without us. When I say we know, I mean there is such a knowledge within our reach which we cannot miss, if we will but apply our minds to that.[161]

The Lockian scheme is straightforward. That there is a God is a "truth according to reason" provable by logical demonstration. Faith then is an assent to divine truths as they are founded upon reason. God exists: and in believing this people have, at the very least, exercised their good sense. This Lockean proposal in favour of theistic belief is distilled by Newman, for the sake of counter argument, in one of his *University Sermons*: "Nothing ought to be received as a divine doctrine and revelation without good evidence that it is so: that is, without some argument sufficient to satisfy a prudent and considerate man".[162]

---

[160] Locke, *Essay Concerning Human Understanding*, Book IV, ch. x, § 2.
[161] Locke, *Essay Concerning Human Understanding*, Book IV, ch. x, § 6.
[162] Newman, *US*, p. 260.

Newman's dissatisfaction with the Lockian scheme, and indeed with all of British empiricism, Berkeley and Hume included, is directed primarily at this very point. He considered its implications for the nature of religious faith to be devastating. On Newman's analysis, Locke's insistence on the rational demonstrability of theistic belief had three major defects:[163]

a) It was excessively rational. According to Locke, faith was the outcome of an intellectual argument; and so long as the argument was apprehended and accepted, it was sufficient. It need not involve what Newman called "the whole man"; i.e. the volitional and emotional as well as the rational sides of human existence.

It follows, then, that b) by placing so much emphasis upon the satisfactory exercise of reason, it effectively restricts faith to those who are intellectually capable of following the argument. The cleverer one is, presumably, the greater one's capacity for faith. And if Newman was consistent about anything, it was his desire to validate the religious intuitions of the unsophisticated. "If children, if the poor, if the busy, can have true faith", he writes, "yet cannot weigh evidences, evidence is not the simple foundation on which Faith is built".[164]

And c), the person to whom Locke's argument was addressed was conceived of as an isolated individual, living apart from all social institutions and relations. Locke's believer belonged to no community, adhered to no tradition. This was Christianity without the Church; piety without the community of saints. Newman the high-churchman, the ritualist, the future Roman Catholic cardinal and apologist, would have no part in it.

---

[163] For the following summary, I am dependent upon Basil Mitchell, "Newman as a Philosopher", in *Newman after a Hundred Years*, Ker and Hill, eds., (Oxford: Clarendon Press, 1990), pp. 224-25.
[164] Newman, *US*, p. 231.

To these Newman added at least two additional criticisms of a more general nature:

d) Locke's account of reasoning as it pertained to religious faith was in itself inadequate. It represented an abstract conception of how reasoning should function, and bore no real relation to the way in which concrete individuals actually think. "[Locke] consults his own ideal of how the mind ought to act", Newman writes, "instead of interrogating human nature as an existing thing, or as it is found *in the world*".[165] As we shall see, this critique links Newman to the line of existentialists that stand behind Gadamer's own theory of human understanding.

e) And finally, as soon as attention is directed to the actual convictions of people who exist "in the world", and the very varied ways those convictions are arrived at and assented to, it becomes apparent that they neither are nor could be based solely upon empirical evidence. Religious knowledge, if limited to what could be based on such evidence, would no doubt be dismissed as having been formed upon grounds too weak to be sufficient. Locke may have underscored the need for a coherent, rational account for the *existence* of God, but in the end he has said nothing whatsover about why anyone would want *to worship* such a God.

To more positive effect, and certainly to the advantage of my work here, Newman's criticisms of Locke reinforced one another in his mind in such a way as to generate an alternate scheme. If faith is to be more than merely cerebral, it must involve a person's whole character; and if this is so, then it follows that a description of the evidence in favour of the existence of God ought to be relative to the personal character of the one describing it. Certain "antecedent considerations"—a phrase Newman took over from Butler, and that

---

[165] Newman, *GA*, p. 109. Italics added.

has a certain Gadamerian ring to it—such as the influences of imagination, emotion, previous experiences and the beliefs of one's surrounding community, would, in Newman's reading, imbue such faith in God with a deeply *personal* character. Moreover, these "antecedents" are themselves influenced by the tradition of thought and practice that precedes—and in terms of imaginative resources, *supercedes*—the individual believer who possesses them. This pedagogical influence of tradition, what Newman labels alternatively as the "formation of the character"[166] or "culture of the intellect"[167] (and Gadamer, to be noted below, as *Bildung*), once it is impressed upon the mind, enables the simple believer to assent to complex theological dogma without having to provide a rational defence.

None of this, of course, is to deny the great influence Locke had upon Newman. It would not be a complete exaggeration to say that the grammatical form of Newman's argument for the personal aspect of religious knowledge, not to mention several of the key terms used in the argument, come straight from the fourth book of Locke's *Essay Concerning Human Understanding*. In addition, many of the most important terms used in Newman's theory of development, terms like "impression" and "relations" between ideas, as well as the two main themes of his theory of religious knowledge, "assent" and "certitude", are decidedly Lockean. Locke's insistence upon two degrees of knowledge, the intuitive and the demonstrative, with the former the more "fundamental and certain",[168] along with his explanation of probability as grounded by the conformity of propositions to experience, are to be found in Newman's theory of religious knowledge *without qualification*. In short, it is impossible to understand Newman without seeing the part Locke's philosophy played in the formation of many of his most basic convictions.

---

[166] Newman, *Idea*, p. 131.
[167] Newman, *Idea*, p. 9.
[168] Locke, *Essay Concerning Human Understanding*, IV. ii. § 1.

NEWMAN AND THE GERMANS

In 1859, Newman added to his *Discursive Inquiries* a short chapter in which he entered a few reflections on the problems inherent to the task of laying the foundations for "a science of metaphysics". Here he discusses what was for him a new area of research: the development of German philosophy from the time of Kant to his own day. Unfortunately for my purposes, Newman's research efforts to this end took a place far behind his other abiding concerns. His only real exposure seems to have been a reading, albeit a *thorough* reading, of an extremely poor English translation (1854) of Chalybäus' *Historical Development of Speculative Philosophy from Kant to Hegel*.[169] Newman applied himself to the work with great intensity; his personal copy shows signs of wear and is well marked with underlines and marginal glosses. These marginal notes, in addition to his chapter in the *Enquiries*, allow one to ascertain in a general way what Newman thought about modern German philosophy. Of particular interest for my study is Newman's opinion of the German approach to metaphysics and how much of it, if any, he incorporated into his own thought.

A P Stanley once remarked, "How different the fortunes of the Church of England might have been if Newman had been able to read German".[170] Newman's problem, however, was not with the language—although Pusey's encouragement to follow him into the "vibrant Romanticism" of German literature probably had deleterious effect—but with the message. Newman considered German philosophy to be "bankrupt" for the single reason of its "obstinate assumption that all things must be reduced to *one* principle".[171] He adds in brackets that this assumption is "against my life long conviction". In short, the problem Newman had with German

---

[169] The book was published, with an introduction by Sir William Hamilton, by T & T Clark.
[170] Cited in Mark Pattison, *Memoirs* (London: Longmans, 1885), p. 210. Even in the English version, he only managed the first half of Kant's *Critique of Pure Reason*.
[171] Newman, *PN*, vol. 2, p. 2.

philosophy is its attempt to establish a rational, "scientific" metaphysics. Such a project would be doomed from the start, he thought. Consider this from the *University Sermons*:

> Let it be considered how rare and immaterial...is metaphysical proof: how difficult to embrace, even when presented to us by philosophers in whose clearness of mind and good sense we clearly confide; and what a vain system of words without ideas such men seem to be piling up, while perhaps we are obliged to confess that it must be we who are dull, not they who are fanciful.[172]

What little he may have understood from his reading of Chalybäus was enough to convince Newman that he had nothing of substance to learn from the Germans and their adherence to a "scientific metaphysics", for they followed a method of reasoning that, he believed, could only lead to "unreal" speculation. "I do not think I am bound to read them", he concluded in the end.[173]

And yet, there are indications that Newman was surprised to find in Chalybäus's rendering of German idealism several points of contact with his own theory of knowledge. When Newman reached page 349 of the text, he highlighted the following passage— remarkable if only for its appalling style—and wrote in the margin, "the most important paragraph in the book":

> But this Identity of thinking and of being had, as Hegel stated, as yet only been presented as an assertion and not yet been proved. In the case of Kant, there was yet a dualism; in that of Fichte a subjectivism; while at the same time immediately and beforehand an objectiveness and infiniteness beyond which Me was also recognised, just as much as that subjectiveness, inasmuch as Fichte had viewed his Me before-hand as subjective and finite—an assertion which necessarily involved the above mentioned consequence. This dualism, which had

172 Newman, *US*, p. 210; cited in Anthony Kenny, "Newman as a Philosopher of Religion", in *Newman: a Man for Our Time*, D Brown, ed., (London: SPCK, 1990) p. 101.
173 Cited in Newman, *PN*, vol. 1, p. 229.

> never yet been conquered, was now at once comprehended
> together by Schelling into an absolute unity, into an Identity of
> the Real and the Ideal.

It is difficult to know whether Newman was giving his assent to the general criticism of Chalybäus (likely), whether to Schelling's metaphysical synthesis (doubtful), or whether the comment is altogether sardonic (improbable, given the tone of the rest of his marginal comments). Regardless, and if one brackets the third option, it seems clear enough that Newman disapproved not necessarily of the *theory* of the unity of thought and Being, but of the manner of its proof. As evidence, consider that beneath his marginal comments, at the bottom of the same page, Newman had pencilled in the following: "N.B. In treating the subject of metaphysics, one should begin with remarks on the *assumption* of supposing that we must refer everything to *one* principle".[174] After this passage Newman seems to have abandoned his reading; at least there are no markings of any kind beyond page 353 to show that he continued or found anything of interest.

It is not clear what Newman meant by this last remark. He had always had the conviction that a purely deductive metaphysics, or any metaphysical system of thinking in abstraction from experience, is illusory. At the same time, he recognised the insistent need of the human mind to think its various thoughts in terms of some unifying principle or "view". "When [thought] contemplates itself", Newman wrote in 1860, "it will at once gain the notion of *unity*..."[175] Significantly for my purposes, he describes this unity not as a regulative principle in the mind, but as something that adheres to the very nature of Being itself in all its manifold relations of significance:

> All that exists, as contemplated by the human mind, forms
> one large system or complex fact, and this of course resolves

[174] Cited in Newman, *PN.*, vol. 1, p. 234.
[175] Newman, *PN*, vol. 2., p. 23.

itself into an indefinite number of particular facts, which, as portions of a whole, have countless relations of every kind, one toward another...Now it is not wonderful that, with all its capabilities, the human mind cannot take in this whole vast fact at a single glance, or gain possession of it at once.[176]

By temperament Newman was adverse to a purely *a priori* metaphysics, for the simple reason that his mind inclined toward reflection on the kind of realities we know in and through experience, not through reflective self-consciousness. But several strands of thought among the Germans struck him as peculiarly similar to his own. Jacobi, for example, was marked favourably in Chalybäus' book for describing reason as something more than a "higher logical understanding". Fichte and Schelling were noted for including in the mental life certain "unconscious representations", which were "modifications of the inner man, states of soul which exist...before our consciousness perceives itself as in them". And he applauded Schelling's deduction that these inner states of soul are non-demonstrable and known only to the one possessing them, so that philosophy always begins with an acute sense of self-awareness, "for nothing else deserves the name of thinking but *self*-thinking".[177]

In summary then, it seems the fairest remark to say that Newman rejected German idealism on the whole for what he perceived to be its insistence upon building an *a priori* "scientific metaphysics"—a sympathy, as we shall see, he shares with Gadamer and the latter's favouring of *Bildung* over *methodos*. Yet at the same time, Newman found several points of contact between it and his own thoughts; especially, and again like Gadamer, among its "Romantic" exponents. Overall, however, the influence of the Kant to Hegel line upon Newman's theory of religious knowledge, one must conclude, is minimal at best: a fact that sets him worlds apart from his Prussian counterpart.

---

[176] Newman, *Idea*, pp. 62-63.
[177] A marginal note cited in Newman, *PN*, vol. 1, p. 234.

PART TWO:

Toward a Newman-Gadamer Synthesis

> *They are in us, those who have long since passed away,*
> *as natural disposition, as burden on our destiny, as blood that throbs,*
> *and as gesture that rises up out of the depths of time.*

> Rainer Maria Rilke, *Letters to a Young Poet*

Newman's general objection to Enlightenment rationalism is, as Colin Gunton has said, "that it wants to know too much and so dismisses too easily that which cannot be exhaustively known".[178] "Rationalism is a certain abuse of Reason", Newman writes, "that is, a use of it for purposes for which it never was intended, and is unfitted".[179] It was to a description of these extra-rational "purposes" that Newman turned his discursive energies in his main theoretical works.

Which is not to say Newman preached irrationalism. He argues against rationalism only as against a mode of orientation that denigrates belief, and thus squanders the grand currency of wonder and the "risk" of a "muscular" Christian orientation of action and

---

[178] Colin Gunton, "Newman's Dialectic: Dogma and Reason in the Seventy-Third *Tract for the Times*" in Ian Ker and Alan Hill, eds., *Newman after a Hundred Years* (Oxford: Clarendon Press, 1990) p. 311.
[179] Newman, *ECH*, vol. 1, p. 31.

"taking a stand". "Faith is a principle of action", claims Newman, "and action does not leave time for minute and finished investigations".[180] But this is far from saying the fundamental condition of authentic humanity—i.e. its stance of faith in God—is non-rational. It is more in keeping with Newman's tone to say that rationalism is not enough. Something more is needed.

Newman's unique appraisal of human reason can perhaps best be approached through one of his early poems. In it we see evidence of Newman's central, *hermeneutical* claim that the human mind is active and imaginative in its reasonings. "Substance and Shadow" is a sonnet that declares Newman's rejection of the "mechanical philosophy" of the previous age which was still current in the utopian ideas and programs of British utilitarians. The poem as a whole dwells on the folly of creating idols out of the limited evidence of sense experience; but it is in the closing lines that the real emphasis of the argument lies:

> Know thy dread gift,—a creature, yet a cause:
> Each mind is its own centre, and it draws
> Home to itself, and moulds in its thought's span
> All outward things.[181]

Newman's scepticism in rejecting "viewiness" and the lucidity of Cartesian rationalism is less an uncertainty about human knowledge *per se* than a critical acceptance, based on his aforementioned sensitivity to human finitude, that "real" knowledge must be filtered through a myriad of individual prepossessions—memories, prejudices and anticipations—and is therefore not a matter of infallibility, but probability. "Though a given evidence does not vary in force", writes Newman, "the antecedent probability attending it does vary without limit, *according to the temper of the mind surveying it*".[182]

---

180 Newman, *US*, p. 188. Also cited in Nicholas Lash, *Theology on Dover Beach* (London: Darton, Longman & Todd, 1979), p. 52.
181 Cited in and commented upon by Roger Sharrock, "Newman's Poetry" in Ker and Hill, eds., *Newman after a Hundred Years*, p. 49.

For this reason it can be said that Newman's epistemological
vision was *personal*, even *individualistic*. By this I do not mean that
Newman is a personalist in the sense that "person" is the ontological
ultimate of his system or in any way a fundamental explanatory
principle. He is too much a theist to draw that conclusion. Rather,
what I have in mind is the same kind of subject-oriented account we
saw in Gadamer's hermeneutical appraisal of aesthetics. Newman,
much like Gadamer, sets at the forefront of his epistemology a
phenomenological account of what *actually* happens when a person
comes to know what he or she knows. And his sampling field for this
investigation is limited to one: himself. Newman considers his own
epistemic experiences to be the only proper road toward universal
application. "Truth is subjectivity", Kierkegaard is famous for saying;
Newman's own declaration is equally as provocative, and if phrased
differently, comes to the same effect: "egotism is true modesty".[183]
Precisely what he means by this should become clearer as I proceed.

FIRST PRINCIPLES

The first thing to be said about Newman's epistemology is that its
starting point is the rational and holistic freedom of the self as the
proper mode of human being, i.e. the centrality of the self as a
thinking, willing individual in his or her concrete existence.[184]
Newman conceives of his epistemology in terms related to personal
modes of thinking; he approaches the mystery of human thought not
in any abstract sense, but in the way it is found reflected in and known
through the medium of the person. Thus his phenomenological
attention is focused predominantly upon the individual; which is to
say, predominantly upon himself. In writing on the epistemological

[182] Newman, *US*, p. 193. Italics added.
[183] Newman, *GA*, p. 384.
[184] Cf. Newman, *PN*, vol. 2, pp. 5f.

processes that precede "real assent", Newman comments:

> We have to secure first the images which are their objects, and
> these are often peculiar and special. They depend on *personal
> experience*; and the experience of one man is not the
> experience of another. Real assent, then, as the experience
> which it presupposes, is proper to the individual.[185]

According to Newman, human reflection and assent (in all realms
of experience, religious or otherwise) are to be natural, active, holistic
endeavours, arising from "the action of the mind itself",[186] forming
and enlarging the mind in a way that is proper to the uniqueness of
one's personality—inclusive of education, likes and dislikes, tastes,
moral convictions, etc.—as, under the influence of perceived realities,
he or she draws disparate elements of thought into a personally-
projected idea of the whole.

It might be said following this that the tenor of Newman's
philosophy considered *in toto* can be described as a philosophy of
existence, a personal ontology; though as we have seen already,
Newman never ventured very far into metaphysics, and thus never
offered a coherent description of human existence *in abstracto*.
Rather, his is a philosophy conceived precisely in terms of the concrete
self, the self in its conscious experience of life. Ideas thus are said to
exist only in the thinking activity attendant to personal action; their
reality independent of human minds is of a lesser degree. The human
person, as Newman portrays it, is free and autonomous, self-
conscious and reasonable; always perceiving, thinking, reflecting and
judging in ways that disclose a self-awareness over against all
external objects. So much is this the case that Newman's rhetoric can
sometimes make him out to sound solipsistic:

> What is the truth? Why, that every being...is his own centre,
> and all things about him but shades, but a 'vain shadow', in

_____

[185] Newman, *GA*, p. 82. Emphasis added.
[186] Newman, *GA*, p. 330.

which he 'walketh and disquieteth himself in vain'. He has
his own hopes and fears, desires, judgments, and aims; he is
everything to himself, and no one else is really anything...he
has a depth within him unfathomable, an infinite abyss of
existence...[187]

This particular aspect of Newman's thought was later to find
fuller expression in the "action" philosophy of Maurice Blondel, and
indeed has much in common with the kind of existential,
"transcendental analysis" found in Karl Rahner.[188] Here in Newman,
however, the agenda is more restricted: it is only claimed that the
knowledge of reality is to be sought less in abstract reasoning than in
the active thinking, feeling and willing of human existence. We have
within us an "infinite abyss of existence" that draws our focal
attention inward, unconsciously, continuously, even as our more
distal attention is occupied with the world around us. Put another
way, and in more Gadamerian terms, Newman assumes that the
totality of what we know as "real knowledge" is to be found only by
first questioning the subtle, "unfathomable" processes of self-
understanding; by peering into the dark abyss of the self in order to
inquire into its basic constitutional orientation as a self-in-the-world.

Already I can draw a parallel here with Gadamer's assessment of
aesthetical understanding. As a consequence of the historicity of all
forms of understanding, and hence the forestructured nature of all
knowledge, Gadamer asserts that we must correct our "self-
understanding of understanding as it is continually practised".[189] We
must, in other words, reassess the truth-claims of human self- and
world-knowledge in light of a fuller conception of self-understanding
in its temporal-regional situatedness. This situatedness of the self is

---

[187] Newman, *PPS*, vol. iv., p. 82.
[188] Cf. Karl Rahner, *Foundations of Christian Faith* (New York: Seabury Press, 1978), p. 20.
"(Human) experience", writes Rahner, "is called *transcendental* experience because it belongs to
the necessary and inalienable structures of the knowing structure itself, and because it consists
precisely in the transcendence beyond any particular group of possible objects or of categories".
[189] Gadamer, *TM*, p. 235.

the tacit ground upon which all subsequent understanding is based; hence only by beginning there can one adequately state what does and does not make for "certitude" in human knowing. Gadamer's success toward this end is still in debate.[190] Yet it remains valid to say that in an aesthetic-hermeneutical worldview, self-understanding is habitually involved in every act of understanding, even if it does not govern the process. "Heightened theoretic awareness about the experience of understanding and the practice of understanding", writes Gadamer, "like philosophical hermeneutics and one's own self-understanding, are inseparable".[191]

Gadamer has been sharply criticised for layimg so much emphasis on self-understanding, most notably by the Italian philosopher, Emilio Betti. Betti considers it would render reason impotent were it always first answerable to its own pre-given limits of human self-understanding. He argues instead that a "scientific" hermeneutics would allow for a greater degree of self-transcendence than Gadamer's more existential model; and thus would facillitate a greater degree of valid criticism. The German sociologist, Jürgen Habermas, has also criticised Gadamer, and along similar lines. In his debate with Gadamer he turns to Enlightenment models of rationality to suggest that unless reason has within itself a capacity for transcendence, and can rise above its own creations, its discourse will always be subject to certain "ideological distortions" stemming from traces of outmoded and unethical forms of human relations.[192]

---

[190] On the one hand, MacIntyre objects, "Between practice, even intellectual practice, so (Gadamer) asserts, and the understanding of practice there is so clear a distinction to be drawn that the understanding of practice is not itself part of the transformation of practice...Here I stand with Betti in holding that Gadamer partially misunderstands his own book" ("Contexts of Interpretation", p. 46). But on the other hand, it is the non-differentiation of practical and theoretical understanding that Habermas finds central to Gadamer's achievement: "I find Gadamer's real achievement in the demonstration that hermeneutic understanding is linked with transcendental necessity to the articulation of an action-orienting self-understanding"; from Habermas' review of *Truth and Method*, translated in Dallmayr and McCarthy, ed., *Understanding and Social Inquiry*, p. 351.

[191] Gadamer, *RAS*, p. 112.

[192] Cf. Jack Mendelson, "The Habermas-Gadamer Debate", *New German Critique*, 18 (1979): 44-73, for a survey of these criticisms. For further literature on the subject, including Betti's criticism, see Richard Bernstein, *Beyond Objectivism and Relativism* (Philadelphia:

In place of Gadamer's philosophy of *Bildung*, then, Habermas proposes a neo-Marxist dialectical analysis, laced with heavy doses of Freudian psychoanalysis and feminist hermeneutics, as the best means by which to rid ordinary discourse of its "feudal" overtones.

But Gadamer has stood his ground. "The only scientific thing", he writes in response, "is *to recognise what is*"—even if "what is" is something that distorts or otherwise limits human rationality.[193] Gadamer admits, and against the pessimism of Schopenhauer and Nietzsche, that understanding is not *only* governed by self-understanding, as if all our knowledge were but expressions of self-interest and the will to power. But Betti and Habermas are wrong to think that through scientific or dialectical means we can purify self-understanding, as if self-understanding were somehow exterior to understanding proper. It is not; human reason is not in a position of control over and above self-understanding; self-understanding is not *free-standing*; it is not an abstraction, but is intrinsic to one's understanding as a whole. "All understanding is ultimately self-understanding", Gadamer emphasises. "In every case the fact is that whoever understands understands himself, projects himself onto his own possibilities".[194] Understanding then, if not subject to the whims of self-understanding, is always already undergirded by it, i.e. always involves self-projection at some level. A large part of what we understand, when we understand, is ourselves. The shape, range and constitution of our self-understanding, therefore, have an effect on everything else we come to understand.[195]

Newman's epistemology, I want to suggest, affirms this principle, if not in so many words. We have seen that Newman's aesthetic of

---

University of Pennsylvania Press, 1983) *et passim*.

[193] Gadamer, *TM*, p. 466.

[194] Gadamer, *TM*, p. 231.

[195] Gadamer's analysis of self-understanding is dependent on his modification of Schleiermacher's hermeneutical circle. He writes, "Anyone who wants to understand a text always performs an act of projection. He projects in advance a sense of the whole as soon as an initial sense appears. Likewise the initial sense appears only because one is already reading with certain expectations of a definite meaning. In working out such a fore-projection, which is of course continually revised, consists the understanding of what is there". From *TM*., p. 236.

religious knowledge unfolds itself in personalist terms. Knowing is the activity not of a mind in isolation but of a whole, living person, and is as individual in its structure as the person is unique. Idiosyncrasies of "disposition, taste and talents", of emotions and intuitions, of experiences and education, act as the heuristic screen through which apprehension must pass, "modifying" and "personalising" as it does so the act of knowing. In describing his theory of dogmatic development, for example, Newman says about Christian doctrines that they

> expand variously according to the mind, individual or social, into which they are received; and the peculiarities of the recipient are the regulating power, the law, the organization, or, as it may be called, the *form* of the development.[196]

Knowledge then is to be based on as clear a vision of existent realities as the mind can reach within its own lived experience, always with a view toward the limitations imposed upon the knowing act by human finitude. "Everyone who reasons", declares Newman, "is his own centre".[197] "There is no ultimate test of truth", he writes again, "besides the testimony born to truth by the mind itself".[198] And if we are to allow Gadamer to have his say, this "testimony born to truth by the mind", if it is to portray a realistic picture of knowledge must, as we have seen, include as propaedeutic a penetration into the inner workings of the self-understanding as it is effected by history, tradition, the *sensus communis* and *Bildung*.

Newman too feels that epistemology must concern itself first with what is happening in the individual mind as it comes to know what it knows; that epistemology is first of all an investigation into the roots of self-understanding. And what it finds there embedded within human consciousness are "first principles", that is to say those

---

[196] Newman, *DD*, 5. ii. 1. Emphasis added.
[197] Newman, *GA*, p. 344.
[198] Newman, *GA*, p. 350.

fundamental, deeply held ideas about things that find their "application" in personal judgments and actions, and that provide the foundation from which a person "builds" a worldview. First principles are "personal possessions", says Newman, and thus are "more immediately ethical and practical".[199] They differ from person to person because they depend upon personal character, and upon the personally perceived "form of society" one finds oneself in:

> They [first principles] require a very various application according as persons and circumstances vary, and must be thrown into new shapes according to the form of society which they are to influence.[200]

Epistemic first principles are analogous to the first principles of a science, but differ from them in being personal; or rather, they are not liable to criteria of universal acceptance. *In abstracto*, first principles may obtain universal validity, but once they enter individual minds they receive unique treatment according to differences in the range, flexibility and imaginative capacity of the minds in which they reside. It follows then that as philosophy treats of first principles, it must also treat of *persons* and the ways they come to accept and modify those principles.[201]

In one of his *Plain and Parochial Sermons*, Newman makes a clear distinction between personal religious knowledge on the one hand, and scientific knowledge on the other. He stresses here the importance of personal and individual thinking where the former is concerned:

> The case is different in matters of learning and science. There others can and do labour for us; *we* can make use of *their* labours; we begin where they ended; thus things progress, and each successive age knows more than the preceding. But in religion each must begin, go on, and end, for himself. The

[199] Newman, *DD*, 5. ii. 9.
[200] Newman, *DD*, 2. i. 3.
[201] Cf. J H Walgrave, *Newman the Theologian*, pp. 114-123.

religious history of each individual is as solitary and complete
as the history of the world.[202]

So at least in the case of religious knowledge, it is inevitable,
according to Newman, that whatever we actually hold to be true, we
hold *ultimately* because we think in terms of certain root "principles"
or convictions we have personally "realised" or "assimilated". These
are so intimate to our thinking and knowing that they are part and
parcel of our very being; they are our "world", our "horizon of
understanding" through which we screen our experiences. Without
this horizon in place we would have no real experiences to speak
of.[203] Without the forestructuring allowed by our first principles, in
fact, we would be unable to think at all; with them in place, all our
thinking assumes a *personalised* tone and shape.

Furthermore, both the adoption of first principles by individual
minds, and the reasoning based upon them, are actions that are
performed at such a deep level in the psyche that, though fully
cognitive processes, under the aegis of the active intellect they remain
tacit and inarticulate:

> It is the mind itself that detects them [first principles] in their
> obscure recesses, illustrates them, establishes them, eliminates
> them, resolves them into simpler ideas, as the case may be.
> The mind contemplates them without the use of words, by a
> process which cannot be analysed.[204]

Certainly there are some principles commonly held by all that can
be identified, such as that our senses can for the most part be trusted;

---

[202] Newman, *PPS*, vii, p. 248.

[203] This runs parallel to Michael Polanyi's discussion of tacit integration in which the
subsidiary and normally unconscious particulars of our knowing acts are brought out of hiding and
into focal awareness. Having done this we can then "assimilate" them into our noetic framework
which itself undergoes alteration as we do so—a type of fusion of horizons. This leads, however,
not merely to an alteration of language, but to a real transformation in conceptual understanding.
Cf. Polanyi, *Personal Knowledge*, p. 111.

[204] Newman, *GA*, p. 282.

that our memories are generally reliable; that the testimony of others is to be accepted unless it can be successfully discredited.[205] Such principles belong to that realm of public discourse in which we are prereflectively immersed, as attested by the fact that we cannot deny them without at the same time presupposing them. By the same token, they have a common, universal validity and do not simply reflect the temper of particular minds. Newman is thus unconcerned about these sorts of principles. True to form, he frames his argument along strictly religious lines. The first principles he wishes to draw attention to are (among others): a personal belief in God, in the truth of orthodox Christian teaching, and in the sacramental efficacy of the Catholic church. Newman is dealing, in other words, at the level of *private* discourse, and wishes therefore to demonstrate to religious rationalists that even their most treasured universal claims arise within particular minds at particular times and places, and as such cannot be accounted for by straightforwardly "scientific" means alone.

Does this singular emphasis upon *personal* belief disqualify Newman from a comparison to Gadamer who, as we have seen, puts so much weight upon *communal* consensus? It might for some who consider Newman to tread too dangerously close to a self-entrenched, self-sufficient individualism. But I want to argue that despite his religious intentions, which admittedly assume a solipsistic pose, Newman retains an acknowledgement of the socio-cultural situatedness of first principles, and that his theory therefore has significant points of contact with Gadamer's account. "All of us have the power of abstraction", says Newman, and thus despite our predilection to configure our knowledge in personal terms, on the strength of this capacity of transcendence we all may participate freely in that "common measure of minds" shared by the various communities we find ourselves in. Furthermore, as he reckons in *Grammar of Assent*, this participation is itself a kind of cognitive first

---

[205] Cf. Basil Mitchell, "Newman as a Philosopher", in Ker and Hill, eds., *Newman After a Hundred Years*, pp. 231f.

principle, as foundational for religious knowledge as religious experience itself:

> Though for one and all of us to assent to the notions which we thus apprehend in common, is a further step, as requiring the adoption of a common stand-point of principle and judgment, yet this too depends in good measure on certain logical processes of thought, with which we are all familiar, and on facts *which we all take for granted*.[206]

Thus, even though assent and judgment are, as we shall see, preëminently (and ultimately) private operations, they depend in a fundamental way on a shared, communal body of knowledge that for the most part is "taken for granted". Individual thought, therefore, while often emerging with its own, seemingly independent and personal configuration, remains nonetheless rooted to a world of commonly-held principles—not unlike what we saw of Vico's theory of archaic language forms. This does not in any way negate the creative *originality* of individual thought; for as Jan Walgrave comments, such "social influences" are in Newman's description "sifted, purified, personally assimilated, and adapted in the process of self-making".[207]   Still, we cannot escape the social roots of knowledge. The world that surrounds us and in which we discover our existence is inextricably a part of our being, says Newman. It is *in us* as much as we find ourselves at home *in it*. Moreover, and in full agreement with Gadamer, he asserts that far from limiting thought, the world's influence upon human self-understanding is a *positive* phenomenon: it serves "to enlarge" our mind; or in one of his better known metaphors (stolen from Wordsworth), "to rearrange our mind's furniture". Consider the following from one of Newman's last *University Sermons*, bearing in mind what I said above about Gadamer's notions of *Bildung* and the "fusion of horizons":

---

[206] Newman, *GA*, p. 82. Italics added.
[207] J H Walgrave, *Unfolding Revelation*, p. 35.

> Again, what is called seeing the world, entering into active life, going into society, travelling, acquaintance with the various classes of the community, coming into contact with the principles and modes of thought of separate parties, interests, or nations, their opinions, views, aims, habits, and manners, their religious creeds and forms of worship,—all this exerts a perceptible effect upon the mind, which it is impossible to mistake, be it good or be it bad, and which is popularly called its enlargement or enlightenment.[208]

I will have occasion to return to this formulation when discussing the relationship between Newman's theory of "development" and Gadamer's theory of "fusion". For now it is important to note that Newman's portrayal of first principles does indeed have an objective element—i.e. that the first principles that structure and orient human cognition are dependent for their existence and "enlargement" on sources *outside* the self—and it is therefore wrong to characterise him, as at least one scholar has, as "a religious individualist, and next to God the world's greatest solitary".[209]

With this in mind, I want now to compare Newman's theory of first principles to Gadamer's reappraisal of the notions of prejudice and tradition. As we have seen, Gadamer claims that understanding always involves a projection of meaning onto perceptions in such a way that our knowledge of things is in itself an interpretative act. In addition, as both Heidegger and Gadamer have affirmed, the sort of personal interpretations involved in the knowing process are themselves rooted in the knower's historical situatedness. From the surrounding historical tradition the knower has unconsciously appropriated certain "tastes" and "judgments"—i.e. "prejudices"— which in turn "fore-structure" his or her subsequent understandings.

Understanding is thus dependent on projection, and hence upon

---

[208] Newman, *US*, p. 284 (sermon xiv. 13).

[209] "Der religiöse Individualist, der grösste Einsame vor Gott": this is but one of the medley of similar verdicts passed on Newman which Läpple has collected and listed in his book *Der Einzelne in der Kirche*, and which Dr. Franz Willam has quoted in his article, "Die Philosophischen Grundpositionen Newman" in *Newman-Studien*, III Folge (Nürnberg: 1957), p. 112.

the prejudices that precede projection as its orientating medium.[210] What one projects are "anticipations of meaning", *praejudicata opinioni*, which guide one's epistemic entré into what it is one wants to understand. This orientation takes place, as we have seen, when a projection tries to "anticipate" a meaning for "the whole" of what is to be understood *before* actually arriving at it. Which is to say that the knower projects in advance what he or she *already* knows of the thing so that further, perhaps more accurate investigation can proceed. A meaning is tried out, so to speak, to see if it fits. If it does, one can say that one has "understood". And if it does not, the knower at least has a starting point, a disposable hypothesis he or she can now seek to overcome. To put this negatively, if the knower waits passively for meaning without anticipating it, none will appear.

Which is to say, there is no way to know in advance whether a projected pre-judgment or anticipation of meaning is appropriate or inappropriate. No amount of *a priori* speculation can guarantee projectional accuracy. There is only one way to find out whether or not a prejudice is legitimate: it must be *projected*, the conviction must be *performed*, the belief must be lived out *as if* it were real. We must be careful, therefore, always to perform our projections with a certain Socratic restraint, for they may fall flat; we must be "tactful" in staging our prejudiced projections, always holding them open to "disconfirmation".

All of which leaves us in a bit of a quandary; for if we only understand by means of our prejudices, we can only understand *truthfully* in light of *appropriate* prejudices. If we cannot get beyond a prejudiced orientation toward the world, as Enlightenment rationalists thought we could, and if in the end we would wish to have understood *the truth*, then we must find a way to make sure we hold the right prejudices. There is no doubt historical conditioning gives rise to false prejudices; hence the pejorative meaning of the term as it

---

[210] Cf. Gadamer, *TM*, pp. 235-273; and Joel Weinsheimer, *Gadamer's Hermeneutics*, pp. 164f.

is ordinarily used. But if it also gives rise to true prejudices, then we can say that in at least some cases prejudices can be productive of real knowledge. The key, therefore, is to find criteria by which to judge those prejudices we do hold; or alternatively (as *per* Gadamer whose polemic goes against the establishment of fixed criteria), to point out ways in which we *naturally discriminate* between true and false prejudices, even if we are not consciously involved in acts of critical judgment. We have seen Gadamer's response to this in his principles of anticipation, application and dialogue, and concurrently the problems that arise from them. Newman, as we will see, motivated by the same concern, comes up with similar solutions and, consequently, similar problems.

ANTECEDENT PROBABILITIES

In his *Grammar of Assent*, Newman is at pains to defend the right of the ordinary non-intellectual believer to possess a *reasonable* faith—this is the point of his famed example, among others, of the factory girl.[211] Newman wishes to represent the faith of simple believers as reasonable even if, owing to a lack of descriptive vocabulary, they are unable to articulate the steps that led to that faith. He maintains that in the lives of ordinary believers there is a real, intuitive grasp of the intellectual and moral fundamentals of Christian belief that *could* be identified and articulated, but that generally is not.

Such "faint reflections" of religious realities as are capable of being perceived can still effect assents to notions like the existence of a "Personal God" who is "immense" yet "incomprehensible", and even to the rudiments of the Trinity when its dogmatic formulation is

---

[211] Newman, *GA*, p. 202; and cf. *LD*, xv. p. 381: "If I have brought out one truth in anything I have written, I consider it to be the importance of antecedent probability in conviction. It is how you convert factory girls as well as philosophers...This has been my feeling both when I wrote of development...and on University education".

broken down into comprehensible bits. On the latter point, Newman asserts that if one is able to understand each individual part of the doctrine—God is one; God is revealed in three persons; the three persons are of one substance, etc.—the human mind's own innate capacities can take over to unify these under the guidance of a first principle like, "What the church teaches about God is true". In this way, even people without the occupational leisure of religious professionals can reach a point where a complex dogma like the Trinity can, in its entirety, be "embraced...with an assent as genuine and thorough as any real assent can be", even if they are unable to render an account for their conviction.[212]

This leads Newman to speculate on the nature of sound judgment: its causes and the things that keep it on track. In general, Newman wants to say that all true judgments, not only those in the field of religion, characteristically occur on the basis of an accumulation of confirmations such as cannot be reduced to rule. One assents first to one bit of a doctrine, then to another; and soon enough, having been emboldened by personal experience and the experiences of one's surrounding community, one finds oneself embracing the whole. Religious belief, Newman argues by extension, functions in a similar way. He describes the manner in which religious evidence, backed by personal religious experience and the witness of the community of faith, converges asymptotically on one's sentiments, ever moving one toward an assent to the whole, though never attaining to the certitude of an *absolute* view of its divine subject (i.e. the innate being of God):

> We know that a regular polygon, inscribed in a circle, its sides being continually diminished, tends to become that circle, as its limit; but it vanishes before it has coincided with the circle...In like manner, [religious belief]...is foreseen and predicted rather than actually attained; foreseen in the number and direction of accumulated premises, which all converge to it, and as the result of their combination, approach it more

---

[212] Newman, *GA*, pp. 111-17.

nearly than any assignable difference, yet do not touch it logically...on account of the nature of its subject matter, and the delicate and implicit character of...the reasonings on which it depends.[213]

I want to move my analysis now in the direction of a comparison of this Newmanian description of "antecedent probability" with Gadamer's principle of "anticipation". We have seen that Newman treats of the inability of human reason to "think or act" without the acceptance of certain "truths, not intuitive, not demonstrated, yet sovereign".[214] Such "first principles" give rise to the development of corollary principles, but these later developments are most likely not in the purview of the believer at the time of his or her assent to the original proposition. For example, one might comprehend the dictum "truth is a duty" without knowing initially the "multiplicity of propositions" that lie hidden within that simple sentence. "No mind", says Newman, "however large, however penetrating, can directly and fully by one act understand any one truth, however simple".[215] One can only procede on the strength of a trust in the rightness of the "truth"; and that over time, by living one's life in its light, by testing it against the hard facts of daily experience, one will be able to affirm the *fullness* of what one had priorly assented to in relative ignorance. With respect to religious belief, Newman writes,

> If we really believe that our Lord is God, we believe all that is meant by such a belief....In the act of believing it, we forthwith commit ourselves *by anticipation* to believe truths which at present we do not believe, because they have never come before us—we limit the range of our private judgment in prospect by the conditions, whatever they are, of that dogma.[216]

---

[213] Newman, *GA*, pp. 320-21.
[214] Newman, *GA*, p. 150.
[215] Newman, *GA*, p. 130.
[216] Newman, *GA*, p. 130. Emphasis added.

There are questions raised by this formula, of course, for it seems to leave us in the same conservative quagmire Gadamer's doctrine of tradition left us in; i.e. that one only anticipates truths after assenting to a dogma one uncritically trusts to be true—here, in this case, "our Lord is God". One is to "limit the range" of one's "private judgment", Newman tells us, only in light of that trust.   This is not unlike Gadamer's insistence upon a Socratic *docta ignorantia* when we are faced with the greater universality of the traditions that surround us, and to whose authority we must submit.   But as we have seen, Gadamer's conservativism is of a more subtle nature than my simplification here allows. Is Newman's equally as subtle? Perhaps, but I must bracket the question for now. At issue for the moment is what Newman means by "anticipation", which he illustrates with the following example:

> I may know London quite well, and find my way from street to street in any part of it without difficulty, yet may be quite unable to draw a map of it. Comparison, calculation, cataloguing, arranging, classifying, are intellectual acts subsequent upon, but not necessary for, a real apprehension of the things on which they are exercised.[217]

Thus it is possible to *know* a thing, Newman says in effect, without having the kind of acquaintance with it logical or formal reasoning may require. One of the most famous historical examples for this kind of knowing is Newman's aforementioned argument from conscience to a knowledge of God. In it we see something that comes close to Gadamer's description of the "projection" of meaning onto things:

> Conscience does not repose upon self, but vaguely reaches forward to something beyond the self, and dimly discerns a sanction higher than the self for its decisions, as is evidenced in that keen sense of obligation and responsibility.[218]

---

[217] Newman, *GA*, p. 115.

Newman calls this kind of knowing by various terms—"real", "imaginative", "apprehensive", "intuitive", etc.—each with a variety of possible meanings and uses; and so it would be a mistake to construct from his thought anything as systematic as what Gadamer presents. It would be equally mistaken to identify Newman's understanding of "anticipation" with that of Gadamer's in any sort of comprehensive sense, for the latter is based upon a hermeneutical insight—the constitutional "openness" of human existence to its linguistically mediated world—which never came within Newman's purview (nor should we expect it to have).[219] Newman the religionist is much more concerned to show the openness of the human soul toward *God*, than to stress any sort of semantic connection between humans and the world that surrounds them.

And yet the similarities become more evident as Newman explains further his principle of "antecedent probability". At the heart of this principle is the difficulty we often experience in trying to articulate the process by which we proceed from evidence to conclusion. In some extreme cases, a person may not even be capable of stating what the evidence itself is. A country farmer, for example, who successfully divines the weather may not be able to give the reasons for his predictions, or may even give the wrong reasons. "His mind does not proceed step by step", writes Newman, "but he feels all at once and together the force of various combined phenomena, though he is not conscious of them".[220] In a similar manner, doctors of medicine are often able to render correct diagnoses without being able to defend them against opposing views. Here Newman again finds a parallel in the work of Michael Polanyi who speaks of the diagnostician's skill being "as much an art of doing as it is an art of knowing".[221] The

---

[218] Newman, *GA*, p. 99.

[219] For a contrary argument, see Franz Willam, *Die Erkentnislehre Kardinal Newmans: Systematische Darlegung und Dokumentation* (Frankfurt: Verlag Gerhard Kaffke, 1969) who claims that Newman's use of the antecedent probability doctrine runs parallel to Husserl's "*Horizont des Verstandnisses*" and to Bultmann's "*Vorverständnis*", this latter being developed from Heidegger's conception of "fore-understanding" (p. 198).

[220] Newman, *GA*, p. 214.

point is that such knowledge can neither be logically demonstrated nor articulated in speech. For "the mind", writes Newman,

> ranges to and fro, and spreads out, and...passes on from point to point, gaining one by some indication, another on a probability...and thus it makes progress not unlike a clamberer on a steep cliff, who, by quick eye, prompt hand and firm foot, ascends how he knows not himself, by personal endowments and by practice, rather than by rule, leaving no track behind him, and unable to teach another...It is a way which [he] alone can take; and its justification lies in [his] success.[222]

Such a description of rational progress has brought criticism upon Newman for his implicit dismissal of logical reasoning, his seeming bow in the direction of utilitarianism—that "justification lies in success"—and perhaps rightly so.[223] But I agree with Hugo Meynall that this does not reduce the strength of Newman's argument.[224] If the work of Karl Popper, Thomas Kuhn and Polanyi (in addition to Gadamer) have taught us anything, it is that the business of explicating theories, methods and hypotheses in any area of inquiry is a matter that cannot always be reduced to simple logic.[225] It is questionable, then, whether the processes of reason with which Newman is concerned would be any better treated by logic and method. Meynall summarises Newman's general argument as follows:

> One ought to be content, in religion as elsewhere, with a convergence of many little confirmations, interlocking and

---

[221] Polanyi, *Personal Knowledge*, p. 54.

[222] Newman, *US*, p. 252-53.

[223] Cf. Jay Newman, *The Mental Philosophy of John Henry Newman* (Dallas: Waterloo Press, 1986), pp. 136-38. The author cites Johannes Artz for the opinion that Newman does not undervalue logically formulated proof, and N D O'Donoghue for the view that he does.

[224] Hugo Meynell, "Newman's Vindication of Faith in the *Grammar of Assent*", in *Newman After a Hundred Years*, pp. 249-50.

[225] Cf. Karl Popper, *Objective Knowledge* (Oxford: Oxford University Press, 1972); Thomas Kuhn, *The Structure of Scientific Revolutions* (Chicago: Chicago University Press, 1962); and Michael Polanyi, *Personal Knowledge* (Chicago: University Press, 1958).

> mutually supporting, none by any means indisputable in itself,
> but properly carrying conviction in aggregate.[226]

Is this not relativism, however? Does it not admit of the same inaccessibility to fixed criteria for judgment that led Gadamer to apotheosise tradition, and Newman, as we have seen, to do the same to religious dogma? For the more we employ cumulative and therefore personally evaluated forms of argumentation in developing our religious convictions, and the more credence we give to personal experience and judgment in marking such arguments as relevant or not, the more bound we will be to confess our knowledge as inextricably influenced by the particular cast of mind we possess and the traditions in which we stand. In other words, the more emphasis we put upon the personal nature of religious knowledge, the more likely we will want to agree with Gadamer that "all understanding is self-understanding", and therefore bound inextricably and beyond redemption to the situatedness of the knower.

Before venturing to argue for the validity of dogmatism, however, Newman first tries a subtler approach. He first insists that God has created in us certain innate tendencies or dispositions to believe that make themselves felt in our actual beliefs. In summary form, Newman contends that there is a kind of religious and moral sensibility—i.e. "conscience"—universal among humankind that, despite its atrophy with disuse, makes us aware of God as creator and judge.[227]

At first glance, this teaching has points of contact with Gadamer's ontological stance that I outlined above, i.e., an innate "openness" to Being as requisite to knowing, but which must be recovered from its forgottenness and brought back into the forefront of consciousness. In the end, however, Newman locates the *telos* and perfection of this

---

[226] Hugo Meynell, *Newman After a Hundred Years*, p. 250.

[227] Newman, *GA*, pp. 303f. As Newman writes, "Conscience too, teaches us, not only that God is, but what He is; it provides for the mind a real image of Him, as a medium of worship; it gives us a rule of right and wrong, as being His rule, and a code of moral duties...and its cardinal and distinguishing truth is that he is our Judge" (p. 304).

innate tendency not in the infinite realm of human possibilities, but in what he deems to be the one and only possibility for human authenticity; namely, the "infallible" teaching authority of the Roman Catholic Church. Newman holds that in guarding against the erratic nature of human sensibilities, Roman Catholicism and its magisterium fixes once and for all time the appropriate "prejudices" that articulate God's nature and purposes for humanity.[228] And "it is here", to usurp E M Forester's words about T S Eliot, "that [Newman] becomes unsatisfactory as a seer".[229]

I say "unsatisfactory", because in bringing Gadamer's thought to bear on all of this, it becomes clear that Newman's own "prejudices"—his religious upbringing, his strong psychological need for closure, his love of controversy, his self-sacrificing journey into the Catholic "fold"—are here being projected as a kind of *ressentiment* onto the evidence without any kind of *Aufhebung*; i.e. without allowing for the hermeneutical reversal that brings a revision, or possible dismissal, of what is found to be groundless. The real question Newman ought to be asking is: why is such and such a revelation, leading in such and such a direction, to be expected given the nature of the testimony we have at our disposal?[230]

And in fact Newman does pose this question; and answers it, if not to satisfaction, with his well-known theory of development to which I want now to turn.

---

228 Cf. Newman, *GA*, p. 131. "To her (the Catholic Church) is committed the care and the interpretation of revelation. That the Church is the infallible oracle of truth is the fundamental dogma of the Catholic religion". Cf. *DD*, 2. ii, where Newman argues, unconvincingly if coherently, for the infallibility of the magisterium as a natural development of the growth of doctrine in the early church.

229 E. M. Forester, *Commonplace Book*, p. 266. This appears to be Colin Gunton's conclusion as well: "As the modernist fashion takes its course, Newman's protests against rationalism appear more and more justified. With the benefit of another century of debate, however, it is also apparent that the mere assertion of dogma is an inadequate response to the crisis"; in Colin Gunton, "Newman's Dialectic", p. 321. It is certainly the published opinion of Maurice Wiles.

230 Newman, *GA.*, p. 214.

THEORY OF DEVELOPMENT

It used to be argued, albeit in a somewhat superficial manner, that Newman's theory of development represents the application to religion of the general philosophies of "progress" or "evolution" that had swept through Europe at the end of the eighteenth and throughout the nineteenth centuries, and that had by the time of Newman's writing of his *Essay on Development* planted themselves firmly in the academic curriculum. At the heart of this philosophy was a revolutionary view of history. It sought to reconcile the sharp dichotomy left by eighteenth century rationalists between the present and the past. Best represented by Hegel, this philosophy espoused the view that history follows a course of development that embodies principles higher than those of merely human reason. According to Hegel, historical change was to be framed not by the theory of a discontinuous progression from one idea to the next, but by the notion of an emergent rational principle that continuously extends itself into the historical flux, then folds back upon itself in new and progressive ways. Hegel's philosophy of history thus allowed for both continuity and a real, historical change for the better. As the British Hegelian, R.G. Collingwood describes it, the "movements" of history travel in "upward spirals, and apparent repetitions are always differentiated by having acquired something new".[231]

Newman, it was said formerly, in accepting this prevailing notion of progress used it to argue—or perhaps convince himself—that the Church of Rome had not *corrupted* the Christian tradition, but rather *improved* it with age. Such pundits focused on Newman's famous assertion that immutability is a sign of lifelessness;[232] and more explicitly, that "to live is to change, and to be perfect is to have

---

[231] R. G. Collingwood, *The Idea of History* (New York: Oxford University Press, 1956), pp. 114-115. Collingwood gives the following example: "Thus wars reappear from time to time in history, but every new war is in some ways a new kind of war, owing to the lessons learnt by human beings in the last one".

[232] Owen Chadwick, *From Boussuet to Newman* (Cambridge: Cambridge University Press, 1987), p. 96.

changed often".[233] Newman's implicit Hegelianism was seen thus as a kind of closet liberalism: "What [Newman] does", wrote James Mozley, Newman's brother-in-law and Anglican critic, "is to assert the old ultra-liberal theory of Christianity, and to join the Church of Rome".[234] Another commentator used language stronger still: "It is German infidelity communicated in the music and perfume of St. Peter's; it is Strauss in the garment and rope of the Franciscan...Mr. Newman is travelling to Germany by way of Italy".[235]

But how is it possible, asked F L Cross in a 1933 essay that first questioned this interpretation, that the arch-enemy of liberalism should have "borrowed...from a liberal source"?[236] Newman's theory of development, Cross argues, like all of Newman's theories, is concerned not with the adaptation of a prevailing philosophy, but with the solution to a concrete theological problem. Newman needed to account for the overwhelming evidence which shows that over the centuries, Christianity has undergone radical change. And his solution, asserts Cross, came not from the "liberal" Continent, but from the more conservative annals of British empiricism.

Cross's article caused needed readjustment to the prevailing tenor of Newman scholarship. One simple fact, Owen Chadwick reminds us, should have been enough to dispel any hints of Newman's liberal tendencies: "He never believed in progress".[237] "No one succumbed less to the idolatry of material discovery or to the enchantments of scholarly and scientific research". And in none of his many scholarly interests is this more the case than in the area of religious knowledge. One of the eighteen "notes of Liberalism" Newman appended to the 1865 version of his *Apologia* repudiates the idea that "Christianity is necessarily modified by the growth of civilisation, and the exegencies

---

[233] Newman, *DD*, I. i. 7.

[234] J Mozley, *Theory of Development*, p. 226.

[235] Cited in Chadwick, *From Boussuet to Newman*, p. 97.

[236] Frank L Cross, "Newman and the Doctrine of Development", in *Church Quarterly Review*, January 1933, pp. 245f.

[237] Chadwick, *From Boussuet to Newman*, p. 97.

of time".[238] As Chadwick comments, Newman "believed in religious
progress as little as he believed in secular progress, and that was not
at all".[239] It follows that it would be mistaken to identify too closely
contemporary notions of progress with Newman's theory of
development.

Having said this, however, we are still left with a theory of
development that in remarkable ways parallels ideas found in
nineteenth century German historiographies. We have seen how little
Newman was persuaded by German metaphysics. Yet he was living
and working within an academic environment where such continental
words and phrases as "trend", "process", the "evolution of ideas"[240]
and the dialectical "interaction of ideas" were a regular part of
discussion.[241] Furthermore, the above citation from his appendix on
Liberalism can and should be dismissed altogether as mere rhetoric.
As I will show here, Newman was all too aware of the "concrete"
nature of history; and thus he writes persuasively, and in a cryptically
Germanic tone, of the movements of doctrinal development as
relative to the powers and limits of unique peoples, times and
circumstances. If he asserted Christian doctrine could not, for reasons
of its integrity, "progress" beyond its original inception, in terms of its
form, at least, if not its essential content, it was certainly "modified"
as it was handed on in tradition. For Newman, as for Gadamer, the
development of ideas, religious or otherwise, takes place within
certain temporal-regional "horizons" of understanding as those ideas
are transmitted from one historically conditioned community to

---

[238] Newman, *AVS*, p. 223. Cf. *DD*, Introduction, p. 10: "One (of the solutions to the problem of
historical change) is to the effect that Christianity has ever changed from the first and ever
accommodates itself to the circumstances of times and seasons; but it is difficult to understand
how such a view is compatible with eh special idea of revealed truth, and in fact its advocates
more or less abandon...the supernatural claims of Christianity".

[239] Chadwick, *From Boussuet to Newman*, p. 98.

[240] Cf. Newman, *US*, p. 329. "One proposition necessarily leads to another, and a second to a
third; then some limitation is required; and the combination of these opposites occasions some
fresh *evolutions* from the *original idea*, which indeed can never be said to be entirely
exhausted". (Emphasis mine)

[241] Cf. Chadwick, *From Boussuet to Newman*, p. 98; also Walter Jost, *Rhetorical Thought in
John Henry Newman* (Columbia: University of South Carolina Press, 1989), pp. 125-138.

another.[242]

Newman's theory of development thus begins with history. Great movements of history, he says, always first appear in the world as an idea within someone's mind.[243] As the idea catches on and a variety of minds begin to contemplate it, assess its possibilities, analyse the experiences its embodiment engenders, and so on, a variety of its aspects begin to emerge. Any single idea is commensurate with the sum total of its possible aspects, however they may vary in the separate minds of individuals.[244] No one aspect is deep enough to exhaust the full content of an idea; no one term or proposition circumfluent enough to define it. Christianity itself, Newman writes, is itself such an "idea":

> If Christianity is a fact and impresses an idea of itself on our minds and is a subject-matter of exercises of the reason, that idea will in course of time expand into a multitude of ideas, and aspects of ideas, connected and harmonious with one another.[245]

Over time enough ideas and aspects of ideas of and about Christianity accumulate so that "some definite teaching emerges". This however need not be the end of development, for "as time proceeds,

> one view will be modified or expanded by another, and then combined with a third; till the idea to which these various aspects belong, will be to each mind separately what at first it was only to all together.[246]

Note that Newman accords the development of an idea to individual minds, not some non-human rational principle.

[242] Cf. Jost, *Rhetorical Thought*, p. 130.
[243] Newman, *DD*, II. ii. 3.
[244] Newman, *DD*, I. i. 2.
[245] Newman, *DD*, II. i. 1.
[246] Newman, *DD*, I. i. 4.

Development from a scattering of an idea's individual aspects to a unified totality of its aspectual potential is very much a human achievement, not directed by the whims of an absolute, abstract *Geist*. Newman explains further: the reason for the continued development of an idea after its appearance in human minds is due to its dialectical interaction with other ideas, already formulated and well-developed, against which it may compare and contrast itself. Once it has been put into some sort of verbal frame, an idea will be "surveyed" in its relation to:

> other doctrines or facts, to other natural laws or established customs, to the varying circumstances of times and places, to other religions, polities, philosophies...How it stands affected toward other systems, how it affects them, how far it may be made to combine with them, how far it tolerates them...will be gradually worked out...And thus it will, in proportion to its native vigour and subtlety, introduce itself into the framework and details of social life...[247]

Newman here clearly admits that the historical circumstances in which an idea rises to expression act as the essential medium for the development of ideas. The effective forces of history compel an idea into dialectical expansion as "the suggestions and corrections of many minds" and the "illustrations of many experiences" interact with the original idea, causing its subsequent expression to grow as it accommodates the ideological nexus of its surrounding environs.[248]

It is the attempt to resolve the tension between this transformative pressure history exerts upon Christian ideas and the Catholic belief in the immutability of dogma that, as Nicholas Lash comments, rests "at the heart of Newman's theological concern" in his *Essay on Development*.[249] Throughout the *Essay*, Newman is desirous to treat of the "concrete" or "real" aspects of ideological

---

[247] Newman, *DD*, I. i. 4.
[248] Newman, *DD*, I. i. 4.
[249] Nicholas Lash, *Newman on Development*, p. 13.

development—not "deductive demonstration"—and the role a personal apprehension of historical facts plays in that development. In short, what Newman seeks in his hypothetical excursion is a comprehensive "view of Christian history" true both to the evidence of historical research, and to the traditions of the church with which he was about to affiliate himself.[250]

Newman's search, in other words, was for an appropriate *hemeneutical* frame by which history could be "read" in its entirety without either ignoring the concrete evidence of development or compromising the "principle of dogma". "Some hypothesis...all historians must adopt", he writes, "if they would treat of Christianity at all".[251] His attention is thus brought to bear not on the "mere facts" of history in themselves, but on the more abstract task of finding an "interpretative hypothesis" that best accounts for the facts.[252] Newman's prior investigations of historical Christianity in a work such as *Arians* had led him to conclude that the "facts of history" are "not present" in the same way "physical facts are present".[253] In the historical sciences where the senses play little role in making judgments, one must rely instead on "auguries, analogies, parallel cases" and the like; in other words, the historian must rely on implicit evidence and personal, imaginative sympathy.[254] "History is an affair of the spirit, of human personalities", writes R G Collingwood in words not unlike Newman's, "and that the only thing that enables the historian to reconstruct it is the fact that he himself is a spirit and a personality".[255]

---

[250] Nicholas Lash, *Newman on Development*, p. 20. As an Anglican, Newman had defended the *via media* ideal, seeing in it a "solution to the perplexities, an interpretation of the meaning, of history". Even the Catholic Newman had difficulty in giving up such a neat and tidy proposal. In the introduction to his *Essay*, Newman does not reject the *via media* altogether; he says rather that it remains "plausible on paper" even if "unreal" and "impractical" in real life.

[251] Newman, *DD*, II. ii. 14.

[252] Nicholas Lash, *Newman on Development*, p. 23.

[253] Newman, *DD*, III. ii. 1.

[254] When Newman describes history as primarily an act of "realising" the "person or situation", he adds: "" wish to be in possession of that living view of him, which shall be a living key of all...which has been committed to tradition or writing concerning him", in *Oratory Papers*, p. 256 (cited in Lash, *Newman on Development*, p. 34); cf. Newman, *GA*, p. 79.

This being the case, historical interpretation, which is itself situated in history, must of necessity be open to revision. For as one projects one's sympathies and experiences onto the evidence, they must be revised where the evidence fails to correlate. At the same time, no evidence would be deemed correlative apart from its relation to the projected interpretation. For without an interpretative heuristic in place, important data is likely to be overlooked as inconsequential. "Mere facts persuade no one", claims Newman; i.e. they must be *interpreted* to be of value to the present situation.[256] Hence theologians who take history seriously will not only feel the freedom to project pre-judgments onto the evidence, they will also allow their interpretative frameworks to change over time. Development is thus the only logical solution to resolving the tension between the ever-accumulating empirical data of religious experience, on the one hand, and those fixed forms of interpretative dogma that tradition imposes upon that data, on the other.

For Newman, development is a two-fold process: the primary and historically prior form of development takes place with respect to the idea itself as its various aspects emerge over time within the historical confines of concrete minds, cultures, and institutions. The second and subsequent form takes place within the minds of interpreting historians, theologians, or church bodies that are forced to readjust their "views" in light of changing historical circumstances. The common link between these two loci of development is their common dependence upon the historical situatedness of the "idea", whether that idea be an original religious experience or a later interpretative hypothesis codified as dogma. Obviously, Newman's use of the term "idea" is a loose and ambiguous one; thus it is essential to inquire further into what is meant here.

Following on his study of the Alexandrian Platonists, Newman chose to view Christianity as an "idea" that at each stage of its

---

[255] R G Collingwood, *The Idea of History*, p. 170.
[256] Newman, *US*, p. 200.

successive development appears concretely in the form of religious beliefs of particular communities.[257] As Newman writes, ideas have "many sides" that "strike various minds very variously" as circumstances change over time.[258] An "idea" implants itself in the mind that thinks it, in other words; and as the configuration of that mind changes over time—as all historical minds do—various aspects of the idea click into place, resulting in changes of perspective through which the idea is interpreted and expressed, yet which nevertheless remain rooted in the original idea itself. This "incarnational"[259] or "sacramental" approach to the study of the history of ideas led Newman, in a fashion certain to have been influenced by Butler, to the conviction that in every historical epoch the church's creeds and rituals are fitting symbolic expressions, appropriate to that time's maturity, of the eternal "idea" of God. This fundamental discovery enabled Newman subsequently to view the process of dogmatic development as that of the on-going "realisation" of the Christian "idea" in the life, institutions, worship and belief systems of its adherents.[260] In the fullness of time, of course, that realisation would reach its completion; but as long as there is human history, there will be *development*.

Newman's platonism, so remote does it place him from the traditional, "logical" theories of development, is for that reason more alive to the inevitable inadequacy, the "arbitrariness"[261] of verbal forms of religious knowledge that arise out of the tensions inherent to the historical process. Witness Newman's comment about the

---

[257] Nicholas Lash, *Newman on Development*, pp. 58f.

[258] Newman, *DD*, I. i. 4.

[259] Cf. Newman, *DD*, I. i. 3. "I should myself call the Incarnation the central aspect of Christianity, out of which the three main aspects of its teaching take their rise, the sacramental, the hierarchical, and the ascetic".

[260] Cf. Newman, *DD*, II. iii. 4; and *AVS*, pp. 68-72.

[261] Newman, *Arians*, p. 181; cf. Nicholas Lash, *Newman on Development*, p. 59. "Arbitrariness" is a key Gadamerian term as well, having picked it up from Heidegger. The German, *Zweideutigkeit*, connotes the co-existence of two possible and competing meanings for a single object or event. It thus sides well with a hermeneutical approach to history, where the same event might be given a variety of plausible renderings.

introduction of the word *persona* into the formula of the Trinity: "It tells us nothing", he says, for "it is only the symbol of the mystery; the symbol, that is, of our ignorance".[262] "Words are incomplete exponents of ideas" he adds.[263] "They are hints toward, and samples of, true reasoning", but are not to be identified with reasoning itself. Truth, therefore, lies not in verbal formulae, but rather in the more personal and tacit acts of human thought and intuition.[264]

This is the principal reason why ideas are subject to growth. Not being tied down to explicit formulae, they possess a freedom that verbal doctrines do not.[265] Ideas, though implanted within, are yet independent of the minds that grasp them. Hence it is a difficult, "ambiguous", perhaps *dangerous* process to curtail ideas in verbal packages: "Whatever is great", writes Newman, "refuses to be reduced to rule...".[266] Whence bears history witness to the episodic, discursive nature of ideas as they pass through time. Newman calls the effort to put religious ideas into words a kind of "warfare".[267] Theological doctrines in their "respective imperfection", he claims, lie "on different sides of the whole".[268] We theologians, then, who presume to speak about God, must "put ourselves on the guard as to our proceeding",

> and protest against it, while we do it. We can only set right one error of expression by another. By this method of antagonism we steady our minds...by saying and unsaying to a

Newman, *PN*, vol. 2., p. 105.
[263] Newman, *US*, p. 275.
[264] This is reflected in Newman's view of Scripture: "The ideas (of Christian revelation) are in the writer and reader of the revelation, not the inspired text itself: and the question is whether those ideas which the letter conveys from writer to reader, reach the reader at once in their completeness and accuracy on his first perception of them, or whether they open out in his intellect and grow to perfection in the course of time". Newman, *DD*, II. i. 2.
[265] Cf. Newman, *DD*, V. ii. 1 and 2. "Catholic principles (ideas) would be later in development that the Catholic doctrines, inasmuch as they lie deeper in the mind, and are assumptions rather than objective professions".
[266] Newman, *Via Media*, I. p. xciv. Cf. *DD*, I. i. 4; and *US*, p. 317.
[267] Newman, *DD*, I. i. 5. The seeds for this thought were sown by Butler in his *Analogy*: "Length of time, then, proper scope and opportunities, for reason to exert itself, may be absolutely necessary to its prevailing over brute force" (p. 82).
[268] Newman, *STA*, vol. 2, p. 446; cf. *Idea*, p. 453.

positive result.[269]

It is from this Platonic starting-point that Newman can speak of development as occurring at two separate moments. Because the original idea is free and alive, its "vitality" and "life" enable it to continuously spin round in human minds with different aspects of it clicking into place at different points in time. A "living idea", Newman says repeatedly, is one that becomes an "active principle" within society, leading people to "an ever-new contemplation of itself".[270] The greater the idea, the greater the number of its possible aspects. As circumstances change, the "shape", the "colour" of the interpretative framework, because human, itself changes, allowing new receptor sites to open up into which new aspects of the idea may fit and be subsequently expressed.

At the same time, the "process by which the aspects of an idea are brought into consistency and form" Newman also wants to label as "development".[271] There is, on the one hand, an ideational development taking place within human minds, and more broadly speaking, within the collective consciousnesses of communities and epochs. And then, on the other hand, there is a development of expression as these ideas are bodied forth, so to speak, at the level of dialogue, debate and eventually *performance*. It is this second form of development that never loses sight of the inadequacy of human statements, especially statements of religious knowledge; that bears witness to the playful "saying and unsaying" of human speech-acts.

---

[269] An unpublished paper cited in John Coulson, *Religion and Imagination* (Oxford: Clarendon Press, 1981), p. 64. I am reminded here of one of Newman's footnotes to his Athanasius translations, where he writes, "It is sometimes erroneously supposed that such illustrations as (Word, Son, Wisdom) are intended to *explain* how the Sacred Mystery in question is possible, whereas they are merely intended to show that the words we use concerning it are not *self-contradictory*...Here one image corrects another; and the accumulation of images is not, as is often thought, the restless and fruitless effect of the mind to *enter into the Mystery*, but is a *safeguard* against any one image, nay, any collection of images, being supposed *sufficient*". *STA*, vol. 1, pp. 43-44.

[270] Newman, *DD*, I. i. 4; cf. I. i. 6; V. ii. 3.6; V. iii. 5; V. vii. 2; VIII. i. 3.

[271] Newman, *DD*, I. i. 5.

On this latter account, according to Newman, the effort to bring past beliefs or doctrines "into consistency and form" always yields a verbal adequacy that goes beyond, expands or develops, what was said in the original. "We elucidate a text", says Newman of literature, "by our [present] comment...because the comment is fuller and more explicit than the text".272

This last notation of Newman's is remarkably similar to Gadamer's famous claim, repeated several times in his main work, *Truth and Method*, that, "Not occasionally only, but always, the meaning of a text goes beyond its author".273 Although not a Platonist in the metaphysical sense, Gadamer admits that his lifelong study of the Platonic dialogues has exerted a deep influence on his work.274 It is not surprising then that he works with a concept of development not at all unlike Newman's. The terms are different— instead of a "development of ideas" effected by their own "vitality", Gadamer speaks of the "subject matter" [*die Sache*] of past texts or events "expanding in being" in and through "conversation"—but the basic concept, I want to suggest, is analogous. Again like Newman, and despite his otherwise profound reliance on Hegelian dialectic, Gadamer does *not* consider this expansion to be a *progressive* increase; he is optimistic about the epistemic efficiency of human conversation, but not unrealistically so. Rather, the enhancement of present consciousness in its relations to the "otherness" of the past is simply made possible by the sheer "difference" in understanding, the altered shape in horizon, of later ages relative to earlier ones.

Which is not to say Gadamer holds to an absolute difference; he rejects the sort of *Totalität* theory, or "sociology of knowledge", seen in those who would wish (or so he argues) to push their own agendas

---

272 Newman, *DD*, III. i. 3.

273 Gadamer, *TM*, p. 264; cf. "Preface to the Second Edition", and p. 335.

274 Cf. Gadamer, *PA*, pp. 43-45, *et passim*. In an October issue of *Frankfurter Allgemeine*, 1989, Gadamer declared that his work on Plato's dialectic remains "the most independent part of all my philosophical work". On the distinction between Gadamer and Heidegger with respect to Plato, see Robert Sullivan, *Political Hermeneutics: the Early Thinking of Hans-Georg Gadamer* (University Park: Pennsylvania State University Press, 1989), pp. 25-29, 140-46, 176-81.

at the expense of learning from the traditions we have inherited. For even when new ideas appear in human consciousness, and are given expression in new grammars and vocabularies, there is still the smell of past ages about them, argues Gadamer, so strong is the hold of tradition upon our otherwise creative and autonomous forms of discourse. "Even where life changes violently", he contends, "...far more of the old is preserved in the supposed transformation of everything than anyone knows, and combines with the new to create a new value".[275] Time changes interpretative frameworks as they move forward into ever new realms of experience; new "possibilities of being" [*Seinskönnen*] appear within those horizons, and along with them new forms of self-understanding, which in turn enable us to interpret and appropriate our traditions in ever more creative ways. But still, this new understanding, Gadamer asserts,

> is not a superior understanding, neither in the sense of superior knowledge of the subject because of clearer ideas, nor in the sense of fundamental superiority that the conscious has over the unconscious nature of creation. It is enough to say that we understand in a *different* way, if we understand at all.[276]

And yet, if the difference in horizonal frames afforded by the passing of time does not effect a *progression* of knowledge, it certainly opens up the possibility that the understanding of the original will be, for present experience, a *productive* one:

> The important thing is to recognise the distance in time as a positive and productive possibility of understanding. It is not a yawning abyss, but is filled with the continuity of custom and tradition, in the light of which all that is handed down to us presents itself...It is not too much to speak of a genuine productivity of process.[277]

---

[275] Gadamer, *TM*, p. 250.
[276] Gadamer, *TM*, p. 264. Italics added.
[277] Gadamer, *TM*, p. 265. Italics added.

There are further points of contact to be made between Newman's two-fold theory of development and Gadamer's work, and here I want to refer again to the latter's theory of mimesis. We have already seen significant parallels between the two: they both are sensitive to historical conditioning, insisting that interpretation take place within temporal-regional horizons of understanding that themselves are always in development; and that this fact both limits and is the very foundation for the sort of productive growth in knowledge that goes beyond, even if it does not supercede, what was known in former times.

With respect to Gadamer's theory of mimesis, I noted that he turns to the Aristotelian tradition of aesthetics in the hope of recovering the epistemic value of art, and of artists as pedagogues.[278] In this strand, as opposed to the Platonic, aesthetic experience is one in which we *recognise* the truth of what is represented *in* the art-form itself. It is the aim of the aesthetic encounter with art, therefore, to incorporate into one's previous understanding of the "subject matter" the new understanding that art, in all its expansion and elucidation, presents to consciousness. In this "fusion of horizons" lies the ethically transformative power of art, says Gadamer.[279] It presents its objects

---

[278] Gadamer, *TM*, p. 103. Classical aesthetics, as I mentioned above, divides itself into two strands, the Platonic and the Aristotelian. In the former, art is thought to corrupt reality, for it stands in relation to the phenomenal world as the latter stands to the eternal Forms. Because art is therefore an imitation of what is already an imitation, it is even further removed from the truth than the world it is imitating. As Gadamer writes, "Plato insisted upon this ontological gulf...and for this reason considered imitation and representation in the play of art, as an imitation of an imitation". The latter Aristotelian strand, however, is more liberal and in turn liberating. In his *Poetics*, Aristotle makes a much closer connection between the discipline of *mimesis* and the universal Forms. Perhaps because his universals are more immanent, Aristotle allowed for art to be expressive of the Forms directly. It is this strand of art that was picked up by Hegel, and through Hegel by Gadamer.

[279] Cf. Keith Ward, *Religion and Revelation* (Oxford: Oxford University Press, 1994), p. 76. Ward admits that Gadamer's agenda is to promote art as a key agent in the "dynamic change of the self"—a change, he notes, that is of "religious interest". But when Ward goes on to add, "Unfortunately, the lives of artists and art critics hardly make such a view plausible", he confuses the issue. Does Ward want us to believe, by implied contrast, that the lives of the *religious* have the monopoly on virtue (certainly a self-serving tenet)? It seems a safe bet that, for all their reputed anarchism, for all their self-destructive seriousness, artists have caused far less damage to human well-being than those acting in the name of religious belief. In any case, as Gadamer's theory of the "autonomy of art" makes clear, it is *art itself*, not the *artist*, that calls us to change. For a counter view to Ward's, and a positive account of the link between ethics and

to us in such a way that our understanding is enhanced, our conceptions deepened, our sensibilities changed, perhaps even our lives reorientated:

> The familiarity with which the work of art touches us is at the same time and in an enigmatic way a collapse of the customary. It is not only the 'This is you' that the art work discloses in a joyous and terrible shock. It also says to us 'You must change your life'.[280]

Art is therefore a medium of real cognitive development, if not absolute progress. Through the encounter with art one is empowered to move beyond the "arbitrariness" of artistic expression to make contact with the real. Truly not every work of art speaks as clearly to us as to say, "You must change your life"; some art, in fact, is downright incomprehensible.[281] Yet Gadamer's definition does help to explain the kind of experience we are all familiar with whenever we find ourselves "lost" in good movie or novel; when we wander aimlessly through an art museum led only by inarticulate feelings; when the beauty of a poem or song "takes our breath away": the striking contrast of the "otherness" of art to our comfortable worlds of the all-too-familiar alters habitual ways of perceiving, forces us to expand our horizons. We say of the experience that we felt "moved", "uplifted", "overwhelmed"; we might even use religious adjectives like "transcendent" or "mystical". Newman had something of this in view, I want to suggest, when he repeatedly used the Wordsworthian phrase I mentioned above, "rearranging the furniture of the mind".[282]

---

art, see Maurice Friedman, *Martin Buber's Life and Work: The Early Years, 1878-1923* (New York: Dutton, 1981).

[280] Gadamer, *PH*, p. 104. See also, *TM*, p. 79, and *RB*, p. 34, where Gadamer again cites this command of Rainer Maria Rilke's. It is from Rilke's famous poem, "Archaic Torso of Apollo", and records his experience upon seeing the ancient statue in Rome. The full line reads, "There is no place which [the torso] fails to see you. You must change your life [*Du musst dein Leben ändern*]". From Rainer Maria Rilke, *Selected Poetry*, S Mitchell, ed. and trans. (New York: Vintage Books, 1982), pp. 60-61.

[281] Gadamer also speaks of works of art that simply "overwhelm us", that "represent an insurmountable resistance against any superior presumption that we can make sense of it all". Cf. *RB*, p. 34.

In Gadamerian terms, what is happening at such "transforming moments"[283] is a "fusion of horizons" [*Horizontverschmelzung*]— the old encounters the new with the effect that some of the old is discarded, and some of the new taken up and assimilated.

At the same time, art itself is already an expansion of horizon. As representation, the *thing* an art-work represents is "raised as it were...to its valid truth". The "being" of the thing is in the work of art "more than the being of the material represented; the Homeric Achilles more than the original".[284] More what? I want to ask. More its real self, Gadamer answers: "The fundamental imitative [*mimesche*] relationship consists not only in the fact that what is placed there is there, but rather also that it has come into the there more like itself [*eigentlicher*]."[285] This statement is far from being straightforwardly clear; but I take it to mean that artistic mimesis is a "bringing forth of the real" into the realm of the senses—an onto-aesthetic *transubstantiation* as it were—in such a way that its essence exists there more genuinely, more *authentically* than before. This is to say that art makes a thing more than what it was originally, and that more is that it becomes more fully itself.

Gadamer unfolds the *modus operandi* of the *eigentlicher* dynamic as follows. When a thing is imitated in art, it is recognised and represented *as* something, i.e. as something *other than* what it is in its *factum brutum* existence. Monet's *Rouen Cathedral* series,[286] for example, is not identical to the actual building that lies on the Seine. This is an obvious fact to be sure, but it is less obvious to state just *how* the two are different. For what Monet has done in his famous series of impressionistic works is to abstract and highlight different aspects of the cathedral's "mode of being" [*Seinsart*]—in

282 Cf. Newman, *GA*, pp. 61, 141; and Wordsworth, *Prelude*, Book I (1850 version).

283 Cf. James Loder, *The Transforming Moment* (Colorado Springs, CO.: Helmers and Howard, 1989), especially ch. 2, "Knowing as Transforming Event", pp. 35-65.

284 Gadamer, *TM*, p. 103.

285 Gadamer, *TM*, p. 103. Italics added. Cf. Weinsheimer, *Gadamer's Hermeneutics*, p. 109.

286 1892-95: National Gallery, Washington D.C.

this case with the aid of fog, filtered light and strong overhead sunshine—which otherwise lay only *in posse* within the building's material structure. Monet, in other words, has creatively registered the "idea" or "spirit" of the thing as a variety of "impressions" the building makes when viewed under changing atmospheric conditions. He has expanded the ontological horizon of the actual building by representing it with "more reality" than would otherwise be available to a tourist looking at the cathedral in "real life".[287] In this sense, there really is no "cathedral" as a pure, uninterpreted *factum brutum*; Monet has simply gathered together and "placed in the there" [*ins Da gestellt*] or "represented" [*dargestellt*] on canvas what otherwise exists as a series of impressions in the very various minds of those who have given their attention to the building.

This raises again the question of what is meant by "reality" in art, for does not one representation necessarily *restrict* a thing's "reality", in light of the infinite variety of possible representations, and the fact that a given artist can only choose one representation at a time? Is it not possible that the reality of Monet's cathedral may be wholly other than that of some other artist? Of course, Gadamer reasons, for every artist will always portray the thing in such a way that some aspects of its being are highlighted at the expense of others; some may even be "exaggerated" to such an extent that they negate altogether other aspects; or, as is the case with much modern art, the original may in the end be completely "distorted".[288]

But these limitations, Gadamer nevertheless asserts, parallel the very nature of reality itself, and are the driving force behind representing that reality in aesthetic form in the first place. With this in mind, I can now read Gadamer's enigmatic statement about reality

---

[287] Actually, Monet's *Rouen Cathedral* series is a unique case: a cathedral is in itself an artistic representation of certain religious ideas and humanistic ideals. And when "translated", so to speak, from the "language" of stone to that of a brush on canvas, new aspects of those original ideas—the grandeur of God, the infinite creative capacity of humans—open up to the viewer in ways that bring new depth to his or her understanding.

[288] Cf. Gadamer, *TM*, p. 103: "Because (the artist) is pointing to something, he has to exaggerate, whether he likes to or not".

with greater understanding, that "reality is to be defined as what is untransformed and art as the raising up of this reality into its truth".[289] "Raising reality into its truth", I can now say, is a creative, imaginative act whereby the artist illuminates an aspect of the "subject matter" which, previously concealed, discloses something essential about that subject. What is disclosed is "real", even if a thing's reality *as a whole* is limited by its mimetic enclosure. Hence there is need for variety in the artists we choose as pedagogues; for the greater the number of representations, the likelier is "the whole" to surpass the original.

Gadamer's reconstruction of classical mimesis thus presents us with a two-fold hermeneutical dynamic not unlike Newman's two-fold theory of ideological development. There is, first of all, the ontological transformation effected by the artist who recognises in an object aspects of its reality that are hidden for want of a proper medium of expression, and who brings them to light by means of the mimetic form. And secondly, there is an expansion of horizon that occurs in the encounter with the artwork as the observer brings the totality of his or her present situatedness to the artistic representation. In this second moment, the contextual clash of differing horizons of understanding is experienced in such a way that when they are fused, they yield new frameworks by which to interpret both the representation and the thing represented.[290]

Consider by way of example Gericault's famous painting, *The Raft of the Medusa*.[291] It portrays in vivid form the horror and fear of innocent death, as well as the life-enhancing hope in eventual salvation. This in any case is how moderns have come to "read" the

[289] Gadamer, *TM*, p. 102.
[290] Alisdaire MacIntyre, Peter Winch and Charles Taylor all speak in a similar vein about the development of social scientific knowledge, which in many ways parallels this two-fold "double hermeneutic" of aesthetic understanding. Cf. Peter Winch, *The Idea of a Social Science and its Relation to Philosophy*, 3rd ed. (London: Routledge and Kegan Paul, 1964); Charles Taylor, "Interpretation and the Sciences of Man", *Review of Metaphysics*, 25 (1971): pp. 3-51; Anthony Giddens, *New Rules of Sociological Method* (London: Basic Books, 1976) p. 158.
[291] 1819: Louvre, Paris.

painting. In Gericault's own day, however, it was interpreted as subversive political satire and as such was forbidden a showing in France. Here, therefore, we see illustrated the two-fold mimetic development of an object: first, there is Gericault's representation of the original historical event (a tragic shipwreck and rescue) as political farce; and second, the later reading of the painting as expressing existential themes. The difference between the two marks a transformation in temporal-regional horizons that has enabled the painting's tradition to develop.

The first form of mimesis, I may now further distinguish, is fixed and static; i.e. the aesthetic expression of reality established by the artist remains in its mimetic form once and for all time. For this reason an aesthetic piece—whether painting, poem or song—is the expression of an age, forever bound to the historical-cultural tradition from which it arose. At the same time, recovering the original intent of the artist is virtually impossible. Time has moved on, and we thus no longer share the same linguistic field as the original artist.[292] Hence the real dynamism of hermeneutical development is located in the second form, the developing tradition of interpretation. This latter form speaks of a moveable horizon that follows the art-work as it enters various cultures in various historical periods. Each new interpretation establishes a new centre, around which new criticism of the piece is generated.

Newman's theory of development, I want to suggest, possesses striking parallels to this two-fold mimesis theory. There is the first form of development, as we have seen, represented by the verbal expression of ideas, the bringing of their various aspects "into consistency and form" through the mediation of langauge.[293] Nicholas Lash, in *Newman on Development*, has described this first

---

[292] This latter intent was the aim of Schleiermacher's so-called "archeological hermeneutics", in which he claimed one could "understand the author better than he understood himself". Gadamer argues strongly against this on account of the temporal-historical gap between horizons. Cf. *TM*, pp. 147ff., 157ff. 162-74, and 192ff.

[293] Cf. Gadamer, *TM*, pp. 99-107. Gadamer has called this level of development a "transformation into structure" [*Verwandlung ins Gebilde*].

stage as a movement from "implicit awareness" to "explicit articulation".[294] Although this level of development, in religious terms, eventually results in dogmatic formulae, its fixity of form need not belie the fact that the ideas the dogmas symbolise trail behind them the time-tempered, ever expanding traditions that have nurtured them.

Secondly, Newman allows room for the further development of those verbal formulae as changing historical circumstances bring about the need for further clarification of the original idea(s). Moreover, Newman implies that such secondary development is potentially infinite, as there are no signs of the general process of development ever "coming to an end".[295] In his studies of the development of historical Christian doctrine, for example, Newman concludes that he is "unable to fix an historical point at which the growth of doctrine ceased, and the rule of faith was once for all settled"; for the former, even to his day, was still in progress, and at each new stage of growth yielding new developments in the latter.[296]

Having noted a great deal of similarity between the two, however, I now must point out that there are also important points of *dissimilarity* between Newman and Gadamer; and these appear, on my reading, to render Newman's own position incoherent. For as much emphasis as he gives to the ongoing *process* of development of the Christian "idea" over time, in both its initial ideational phase and its subsequent hermeneutical phase; as emphatically as he stresses the "newness" of the expanding aspectual awareness of later ages relative to earlier ones, in the end Newman does *not* believe, as I stated at the beginning, in genuine change. Despite his lip service to the "modification" of ideas, the "deepening" and "broadening" of the "stream" of religious knowledge, the "additions" to the Creed, and the "additions and accretions" to the Christian faith,[297] Newman

[294] Nicholas Lash, *Newman on Development*, p. 78.
[295] Newman, *DD*, Introduction, section 20.
[296] Newman, *DD*, II. ii. 12.

nevertheless maintains without qualification that if the church were ever to change its mind about something it formerly held to be true, the whole foundation on which its doctrine rests would be destroyed.[298] Newman's expanding horizon is clearly not a moveable feast. It is cumulative, even infinitely so; but it is never reversible.[299] And the reason for this, as I will explain below, follows from Newman's *a priori* argument—surprising for one so otherwise sensitive to history—for an infallible ecclesiastical authority.

Having said this, however, it should be made clear that, true to form, Newman only held to an irreversible cumulative horizon in the *religious* sphere. His more general educational ideal was clearly progressive, and thus far more in line with Gadamer's hermeneutical scheme. And like Gadamer's,[300] Newman's pedagogical scheme is based upon an ontology of human "experience":

> Let a person, whose experience has hitherto been confined to the more calm and unpretending scenery of these [British] islands...go for the first time into parts where physical nature puts on her wilder and more awful forms...then I will suppose he will have a sensation which perhaps he never had before. He has a feeling not in addition or increase of former feelings, but of something different in its nature...He has made *a certain progress,* and he has a consciousness of mental enlargement; he does not stand where he did, he has *a new centre,* and a range of thoughts to which he was before a stranger.[301]

What is this if not a *progressive* "fusion" of differing perspectives

---

[297] Newman, *DD,* I, i. 6; I, i. 7; II, ii. 2; III. i. 1 and 2—respectively.

[298] Cf. Nicholas Lash, *Newman on Development,* p. 34. And cf. Newman, *GA,* p. 131, on the infallibility of the Church as the "fundamental dogma of the Catholic religion".

[299] Cf. Newman, *Idea,* p. 272. Of scripture—which is, admittedly, *sui generis* relative to dogma—Newman writes: "Christianity is built upon definite ideas, principles, doctrines, and writings, which were given at the time of its first introduction, and have never been superseded, and admit of no addition".

[300] Gadamer, *TM,* pp. 310f. Gadamer links his philosophy of "experience" to Bacon and Aristotle, and so perhaps these are the common links between him and Newman. Gadamer goes beyond Newman, however, and incorporates Hegelian dialectic, and the Heideggerian critique of Hegel into his theory of experience.

[301] Newman, *Idea,* p. 150. The first set of italics were added, but the second are Newman's.

into a new "view", forming a "new centre", a new horizon around which new critical opinions are generated and old ones discarded? So if in the realm of religion Newman hedges in personal experience with his doctrine of an infallible authority, in a more general sense he seems still close to the Gadamerian line in allowing free range to the infinite process of knowledge—even at the risk that the "productivity of process" may just lead into areas of thought that are decidedly unprogressive.

It is inconceivable, therefore, that Newman and Gadamer could be in such agreement in their respective theoretical arguments for the development of ideas, and in such disagreement about the direction in which such arguments are bound to lead. For the latter, the aesthetic and hermeneutical dynamics of development lead to an "openness" to new experiences of reality and hence to ever-changing formulations of ideas. While the former, in complete agreement with this in every realm save the religious, forces a seemingly incoherent irreversibility upon this last.

I will want to investigate Newman's argument for an infallible authority in greater detail, for it now seems to be the most prominent obstacle standing between him and his incorporation into the Gadamerian coterie of aesthetic-hermeneutical philosophers. Any account of Newman's philosophy would be incomplete, however, without first bearing testimony to what is perhaps his most characteristic, if not most misunderstood doctrine, the nature of personal judgment he calls the "illative sense".[302]

---

[302] What follows is taken from a number of secondary sources in addition to Newman's own account of it in his *Grammar of Assent*. Cf. Newman, *PN*, vol. 2, pp. 78f; Antony Kenny, "Newman as a Philosopher of Religion", in D Brown, ed., *Newman*, pp. 113f.; S Jaki, "Newman's Assent to Reality", in *Newman Today*, (San Francisco: Ignatius Press, 1989), pp. 203f.

THE ILLATIVE SENSE

Despite his adherence to the dogmatic authority of the church in matters of religion, Newman in more general terms was never one to shy away from the risks involved in the great human adventure of thinking deeply about things. One cannot be afraid of lacking certitude for our speculations, said Newman, for our minds are so constituted that,

> if we insist on being as sure as is conceivable, in every step of our course, we must be content to creep along the ground, and can never soar. If we are intended for great ends, we are called to great hazards; and whereas we are given absolute certainty in nothing, we must in all things choose between doubt and inactivity.[303]

This romantic, anti-Cartesian sentiment should not dissuade us from what we have seen Newman elsewhere say about certainty; namely, that while we cannot always explain the way we come to a position of certainty—especially in religious matters—nevertheless, we are able to justify our assents in utilitarian fashion "by their success". So I am led to ask, what can possibly be meant by "success" in matters of religion? On Newman's own account there is little difference between religious faith and speculative assumption. In each case the grounds are conjectural: the issue is a personal acceptance of an idea as universally valid.[304] "Faith", writes Newman,

> starts from probability, yet it ends in peremptory statements, if so be, mysterious, or at least beyond experience. It believes an informant amid doubt, yet accepts his information without doubt.[305]

---

[303] Newman, *US*, p. 218.
[304] Cf. Antony Kenny, "Newman as Philosopher", p. 107.
[305] Newman, *US*, p. 220.

Like Newman, Locke says that there can be no demonstrable truth in concrete matters, and therefore assent to a concrete proposition must always be conditional. Probabilistic reasoning can never lead to certitude in any sort of absolute sense. But unlike Newman, Locke draws from this the conclusion that if certitude exists at all, it admits of degrees, and that an unconditional assent has no legitimate exercise except as ratifying acts of intuition or demonstration. The unerring mark of rationality is the conviction—it would become a watchword for rationalists—not to entertain any proposition with greater certainty than the proofs it is built upon will warrant. "Whoever goes beyond this measure of assent", writes Locke in surprisingly proto-Nietzschean tones, "...receives not truth in the love of it, loves not truth for truth-sake, but for *some other by-end*".[306]

Even though, as I said, he cashes in on its initial claim, Newman makes this doctrine of Locke's one of his main targets of attack.[307] Newman's general complaint is a hermeneutical one: Locke fails to separate assent sufficiently enough from the trail of discursive reasonings that support it. And without doing so, assent is reduced to a mere echo of inference.[308] But in fact the former is not always dependent on the latter. "Either assent is intrinsically different from inference", writes Newman, "or the sooner we get rid of the word...the better".[309] Newman argues that one may assent to something long after we have forgotten the reasons for our assent. And sometimes our reasons are strong, even convincing in an absolute sense, yet we withhold our assent. Coherent argumentation and demonstrable proof, he concludes, are not guarantors of whether a thing will be assented to, for assent admits of no gradation. With assent, like Newman's own to his new-found Roman Catholic loyalties, it is an *all or nothing* proposition:

---

[306] Locke, *Essay on Human Understanding*, IV, xvi, paragraph 6. Italics added.
[307] Cf. especially Newman, *GA*, pp. 136-139.
[308] Cf. Kenny, "Newman as Philosopher", p. 107.
[309] Newman, *GA*, pp. 140-41.

> Very numerous are the cases in which good arguments, and
> really good as far as they go, and confessed by us to be good,
> nevertheless are not strong enough to incline our minds ever
> so little to the conclusion at which they point...We refuse to
> assent at all, until we can assent to it altogether. The proof is
> capable of growth; but the assent either exists or does not
> exist.[310]

It follows, then, that full assent, even in demonstrative matters, cannot in any way countenance doubt. In concrete cases, Newman argues *contra* Locke, there are no instances where we give partial assent of either greater or lesser strength:

> If assent is the acceptance of truth, and truth is the proper
> object of the intellect, and no one can hold conditionally what
> by the same act he holds to be true, here too is a reason for
> saying that assent is an adhesion without reserve or doubt to
> the proposition to which it is given...In the case of all
> demonstrations, assent, when given, is unconditionally
> given.[311]

This does not, however, restrict assent only to instances of demonstrative proof. We all believe beyond a doubt that we exist, for example, that we "think, feel, and act in the home of our own minds".[312] Newman's favourite example of a firm assent based on undemonstrable evidence, and consequently of the impossibility of degrees of assent, is our conviction that "Great Britain is an island":

> They [Locke and his followers] do not, for instance, intend for a
> moment to imply that there is even a shadow of a doubt that
> Great Britain is an island, but they think we ought to
> know...that there is no proof of the fact, in mode and figure,
> equal to the proof of a proposition of Euclid; and that in
> consequence they and we are all bound to suspend our
> judgment about such a fact, though it be in an infinitesimal

[310] Newman, *GA*, p. 143.
[311] Newman, *GA*, p. 145.
[312] Newman, *GA*, pp. 148f.

degree, lest we should seem not to love truth for truth's sake.[313]

For all these instances of truth founded upon *reductio ad absurdum* arguments—truths such as the facts of my existence, my birth and my eventual death—we are able to render an assent without requiring absolute demonstration, contends Newman. And religious faith, he adds, is of a piece with this kind of reasoning. It demands an assent that can neither be "irresistibly" demonstrated nor proved, "else how comes it to be resisted?"[314] "For me", Newman writes,

> it is more congenial to my own judgment to attempt to prove Christianity in the same informal way in which I can prove for certain that I have been born into this world, and that I shall die out of it.[315]

Newman's assent to Christianity, however, will only work for those who are prepared for it, for those whose natural sentiments have been imbued, through religious *Bildung* or *formatio*, with a religious sympathy. "We meet with men of the world", he writes, "who cannot enter into...devotion...because they know of no exercise of the affections but what is merely human".[316] The evidences for the Christian religion, therefore, "presuppose a belief and perception of the Divine Presence". And such a "perception", Newman declares in Gadamerian fashion, is a kind of cognitive "taste" acquired through the "personal influence" of Christian teachers and saints, history and scripture.[317] The grounds for religious knowledge then must "touch the heart",[318] and are not established syllogistically but grow and converge one upon another. They are perceived not by logical inference, but by that personal act of knowing Newman calls "the

---

[313] Newman, *GA*, pp. 151-52.
[314] Newman, *GA*, p. 214.
[315] Newman, *GA*, p. 214.
[316] Newman, *GA*, p. 44.
[317] Cf. Newman, *US*, sermon 5, "Personal Influence, the Means of Propagating the Truth".
[318] Newman, *GA*, p. 323; and *US*, pp. 218, 224.

illative sense".[319]

In his discussion of the illative sense, Newman is drawing attention to two distinct facts. He is concerned, first of all, to make the point that our reasoning is often implicit, informal, even unconscious, but that it is on all accounts still rational. And secondly, Newman argues that our reasoning concerning matters of fact ineluctably involves a personal or subjective element that recognises the truthfulness of non-demonstrable, concrete things, and of which it is vital to the study of religious faith to highlight and demonstrate.

Enough has been said about the first. I want to turn now to the epistemologically more important issue of personal or subjective judgment. The illative sense is, in the simplest of terms, the faculty of *personal judgment*. It is thus, like Kant's critique of taste, exclusive to the subject. "We judge for ourselves", wrote Newman, "by our own lights, and on our own principles".[320] All our acts of judgment are relative to the illative sense and limited, therefore, by the cognitive capacities of our own minds.

It is significant to my purposes to note that in his description of the illative sense, Newman appropriates Aristotle's theory of *phronesis*—practical or experiential wisdom. The illative sense signifies for Newman that highly personal moment in the knowing process that is put into action whenever judgments need to be made. As such it finds a "parallel faculty" in *phronesis*, the function of which emerges in Newman's famous answer to the following question:

> How does the mind fulfil its function of supreme direction and control, in matters of duty, social intercourse and taste? In all of these separate actions of the intellect, the individual is supreme, and responsible to himself, nay, under circumstances, may be justified in opposing himself to the judgment of the whole world...[321]

---

[319] Newman, *GA*, pp. 271f.
[320] Newman, *GA*, p. 230.
[321] Newman, *GA*, p. 277.

We have already seen Gadamer put the doctrine of *phronesis* to good use in his reformulation of the notion of *sensus communis*, as well as to frame his Heideggerian paradigm of self-understanding. For Newman, *phronesis* also bears witness to an experiential form of knowing applicable to "matters, personal and social", and that, like the hermeneutical reasoning of *Bildung* and the *sensus communis*, is impossible to codify or explain to others. Yet he is less concerned than Gadamer to extricate its more processual moment of "anticipation" than to focus attention on what results in the end: namely, personal, subjective judgment:

> [Aristotle] calls the faculty which guides the mind in matters of conduct, by the name of *phronesis*, or judgment. This is the directing, controlling, and determining principle in such matters, personal and social. What it is to be virtuous, how we are to gain the just idea and standard of virtue, what is right and wrong in a particular case...the philosopher refers us to no code of laws, to no moral treatise, because no science of life, applicable to the case of an individual, has been or can be written. Such is Aristotle's doctrine, and it is undoubtedly true.[322]

The illative sense, then, like the judging faculty of *phronesis*, is that highly individualised function of the mind that renders non-demonstrative judgments. It is sharpened and honed by experience much in the same way Gadamer's horizon-motif accounts experience an important result of the engagement of one horizon with another. And because the illative sense is a highly personal function, it is neither definitive nor universal. In short, it relies for its actions upon implicit and inarticulate forms of reasoning. It cannot *explain*, it simply *knows*, what it values.

The end result of human reasoning, therefore—i.e. judgment—is "ever moving in a circle", says Newman, and cannot escape the limits of its own finitude. How then can we ever hope to reach conclusive

[322] Newman, *GA*, p. 277.

decisions about things? How is certitude, to put a Nietzschean spin on the question, ever anything more than a psychologically-projected form of self-approval?

Newman defends himself against these and similar questions; for, as he admits, he is keen to avoid reducing the illative sense to "a mere sense of propriety".[323] Illative judgment is not a case of limiting truth to whatever one happens to like at the time. It is subjective, to be sure, and in itself not absolute; but it is not "untrustworthy". Newman thus sets about defending his doctrine by arguing for its relative *objectivity*, and does so in the following two ways. But it needs to be said up front that despite appearances to the contrary, Newman's ways are *not* Gadamer's ways.

First, one must cultivate a trust that "the intellect, which is made for truth, can attain truth, and, having attained it, can keep it, can recognise it, and *preserve* the recognition".[324] For like Augustine and Plotinus before him, and indeed Gadamer after,[325] Newman believes in the substantial affinity between the human mind and truth.[326] He says in effect, *ala* Gadamer, that there exists a certain "openness" between human understanding and what is the case, a certain pre-given "clearing"—to use the Heideggerian term—which establishes the fundamental and existential ground upon which knowledge is based. Gadamer expands on this notion to speak of the act, like Newman, of "preserving" [*bewahren*] the truth of tradition in one's interpretative application of it.[327] But unlike the Heidegger-

---

[323] Newman, *GA*, p. 277.

[324] Newman, *GA*, p. 272.

[325] Cf. Augustine, *Confessions*, X. xxvii. "Late have I loved Thee, O Beauty, ever ancient and ever new...for behold, Thou wert *within me* and I knew it not..." Italics added; and Plotinus, *Enneads*, I. vi; and V. viii.

[326] I am not yet sure just how much Newman, as an anti-metaphysician, would have agreed to a substantial or ontological *unity* between mind and its objects. Whether Newman believes like Plotinus and the Greek Fathers that the soul is of the same substance as the Divine Logos remains in my mind to be proved. Yet he does at times seem to come close to holding this position.

[327] Cf. Gadamer, *TM*, pp. 255-57, among other examples. Gadamer develops his theory of "preservation" by playing off the subtle semantic connections between the words *Bewahrung*, "preservation", *Bewährung*, "that which has passed the test", and *Wahrheit*, truth.

Gadamer synthesis I described above, in Newman's description the onto-existential affinity between experience and truth lies in dormant potency in the *ordinary* human, and only rises to actuality in the believing Christian, under the aegis of the church's pedagogical guidance. Its substance is the indwelling presence of Christ residing in human minds as the *imago Dei*. Thus what Gadamer holds out as the *universal* foundation for establishing trustworthy truth-claims, Newman makes subordinate to a priorly held belief in a given set of religious doctrines, and only those of a specific religious sect, and thus to the *exclusion* of all those who withhold their assent from such doctrines.

Secondly, and more satisfactorily, Newman defends the illative sense against pure subjectivism by seeking to redefine in more expansive terms what is normally meant by personal judgment. The illative sense is subjective, but it is not an act performed by an isolated faculty of the mind. Like Kant's legitimation of aesthetic taste, Newman claims the illative sense is a "sense" like any other, parallel in function to "good sense" or "common sense" or one's "sense of beauty". It thus stands in relation to our "being", our "mind and body", in such a way that all things on which it passes judgment are "of necessity referred to it [our total being] and not it to other things".[328] It should follow from this, therefore, that the illative sense is also a *communal* sense, for one only has one's personal "being" by relation to other "beings" with whom we live in community. For it would appear that if the illative sense, as Newman says, is a subsidiary function of the whole person as a thinking, feeling, willing unity, and if the whole person is always already embedded in history *and* community, then it follows that it is a capacity possessed by *all* people, not just Christians, even if only the latter put it to its proper use. But again, as we shall see, Newman disappoints.

The point of contention between Newman and Gadamer here revolves around the notion of "certitude". They each believe in it, but

---

[328] Newman, *GA*, p. 272.

each renders significantly different definitions. Following on an analysis of Wilhelm Dilthey, Gadamer distinguishes between "scientific certainty" and "the kind of certainty one acquires in life". The former, in Gadamer's words, "has something Cartesian about it", i.e. it excludes all doubt and does not admit of degrees. But because the latter must bear up under "the weight of historical concreteness", and is at work in the task of understanding more human centred phenomena such as "tradition, morals, religion and law", it cannot be comprised of "an undoubted whole". Its judgments come strictly from "the spirit...[which] produces out of itself valid knowledge".[329] And because the human spirit, for reasons of its historical situatedness, is "ever on the way", its judgments can only be as certain as the strength of its personal commitment to them at the moment they are formulated. Assent in matters of judgment, in other words, admits of degrees—not, as *per* Locke, for lack of demonstrable evidence, but for lack of personal involvement in the issue at hand; and that for reasons too subtle to explain.

In similar fashion, Newman determines that the illative sense represents that state of concrete, life-bound existence in which "certitude" governs our sense of the right and the true.[330] And likewise, what Newman means by "certitude" is something that is derived strictly from within the confines of personal involvement. "Certitude is not a passive impression made upon the mind from without", he writes,

> but in all concrete questions—nay, even in abstract, for though the reasoning is abstract, the mind which judges of it is concrete—it is an active *recognition* of propositions as true, such as it is the duty of each individual himself to exercise at the bidding of reason, and, when reason forbids, to withhold.[331]

[329] Gadamer, *TM*, p. 211.
[330] Newman makes it clear that the illative sense is not an independent faculty, but is part of the overall function of mind in its quest for truth.
[331] Newman, *GA*, p. 271. Emphasis added.

It is important to note that though Newman links certitude to propositional truth, it is not rightly an attribute of propositions themselves. Nor is Newman's conception of certitude, contrary to John Hick's reading of the *Grammar of Assent*, a "propositional attitude".[332] Rather "certitude" is an internal "mental state" that, like the Heideggerian "fore-structure" of understanding, like the Gadamerian rubric of prejudiced self-understanding, *projects itself* onto such statements in which it *recognises* the property we call truthfulness, and to which it subsequently predicates the term "certainty". "Absolute proof" says Newman, "...can never be furnished to us by the logic of words", but is instead *rendered by our own minds*, for "everyone who reasons is his own centre".[333] Certitude, therefore, is a natural state dependent for its existence upon the constitutional make-up of the individual mind and that mind's ability to recognise the truth any particular proposition may or may not contain. The illative sense, by means of projection, merely puts its stamp of approval upon the prior *hermeneutical* acts of recognition. So far, *so Gadamerian*.

And the Gadamerian connection continues when Newman goes on to describe this more interpretative aspect of the illative sense as "the faculty of composition". For by means of this faculty we are able to

> follow the descriptions of things which have never come before us, and to form out of such passive impressions as experience has heretofore left on our minds new images which, though mental creations, are in no sense abstractions, and though ideal, are not notional.[334]

---

[332] Cf. John Hick, *Faith and Knowledge* (Ithaca: Cornell University Press, 1957), pp. 90-91. Hick criticises Newman for assuming faith to be a "propositional attitude"; that faith is "essentially a matter of believing theological propositions". As the following discussion on the illative sense shows, this is not far from the truth about Newman, but it certainly is not fully representative of his views.

[333] Newman, *GA*, p. 271.

[334] Newman, *GA*, p. 42.

What are we to understand by Newman's use of the term "impressions"—here qualified, in anti-Gadamerian fashion, as "passive"—out of which these new images are formed? Clearly Newman has in mind something other than Hume's conception of the "decaying images" impressed upon one's mind by the senses. Newmanian "impressions", rather, persist over time as *memoranda*, and are instrumental *hermeneutically* in the formation of mental images. To illustrate his point Newman gives several examples, the most striking of which is his imaginary rendering of fictional characters:

> I am able as it were to gaze upon Tiberius as Tacitus draws him and to figure to myself our James the First as he is painted in Scott's Romance. The assassination of Caesar, his *Et tu Brute*, his collecting his robes about him, and his fall under Pompey's statue, all this becomes a fact to me and an object of real apprehension.

From this he draws a generalisation, and in so doing seems to qualify his qualification of "impressions" as "passive"; and, or so it seems to me, in decidedly Gadamerian tones:

> Thus it is that we live in the past and in the distant; by means of our capacity of interpreting the statements of others about former ages or foreign climes by the lights of our own experience...[which] derives its vividness and effect from its virtual appeal to the various images of our memory. This *faculty of composition* is of course a step beyond experience, but we have now reached its furthest point...[335]

It seems then that Newman's illative sense, as governing the imaginative capacity of the mind to connect present experience with the mental impressions past experiences leave us with—impressions I can now add that, far from being "passive", lend the imagination its "vividness and effect"—displays a certain aesthetic and

---

[335] Newman, *GA*, pp. 42-43. Italics added.

hermeneutical *modus*.[336]   Whether we are reading a novel, watching a play or forming a judgment about some particular circumstance we find ourselves in, the illative sense acts in each case by using our store of impressions to conjure up mental images of what it is we are interpreting so that it is more readily available to our apprehensive faculties. With this image in place, our illative sense can engage its judging capacity to offer an assessment of the thing's truthfulness, its "certainty", and thus of our right to possess "certitude" about it and give our assent to it. I repeat: this puts Newman's epistemology very close to the way Gadamer has rehabilitated the classical notion of aesthetic mimesis—only this time to an aspect of the doctrine I have not yet discussed; and in discussing it, we will see where the real differences lie.

Gadamer, as I have already shown, is keen to stretch the definition of mimesis beyond Plato's pessimism to include the more cognitive and subject-oriented function of "recognition".[337] He does this in part by connecting it to Plato's own account of *anamnesis*. In the Gadamerian spin, *anamnesis* is defined as a function whereby tacit traces of what was once known but has since been forgotten are unconciously re-collected; and then *projected*, along with our more public prejudices, onto the thing being understood, as that thing presents itself in its own characteristic mode of being. And thus, though we are right in saying that in the artist's gaze a more essential grasp of the thing itself is attained, artistic representation is also, at least potentially, a more essential *self*-grasping. When we say of the art-work, "Yes, that is how things are!", what we are really saying too is, "Yes, *that is how I am!*"

When Gadamer applies this notion to his aesthetics, he asserts that on the one hand, in learning to see a familiar object in a new way through its representation in the work of art, we come to learn

---

[336] For confirmation of this view, as well as a critique of Newman's epistemology I consider to be sympathetic to my own portrayal, see H. H. Price, *Belief* (London: George Allen and Unwin, 1969), pp. 327-330.
[337] Cf. Warnke, *Gadamer*, pp. 59f; and Gadamer, *TM*, pp. 102f.

something new about the thing being represented. An essential part of its being has been highlighted and creatively portrayed, allowing our experience of it to be epistemically productive. For Gadamer, art is truly pedagogical; it "speaks to us of things which in all our endless lives we have not yet found, and perhaps shall never find".[338] On the other hand, in the hermeneutical reversal mentioned above, the apprehension of this newness reflects back upon us; we *recognise* the new vision of the thing as something strangely familiar. Rembrandt's *Nightwatch* and Monet's *Rouen Cathedral* show us things we could not see without them, things we may not wish to see; yet having seen such things, we are forced to admit that what we are seeing in all its newness is perhaps but a neglected aspect of what we ourselves *are*, otherwise we would not be able to "re-cognise" anything there at all.[339] Gadamer portrays this dialectical relation between otherness and familiarity—itself, of course a famed Hegelian doctrine—as part of what he means by the anamnestic aspect of aesthetic "recognition". "Recognition" is literally a "cognising again" [*Wiedererkennen*, lit., "making familiar again"], and as such it marks the most self-involving moment in the whole mimetic process. We only recognise the splinter of truth in art, runs Gadamer's version of the famed metaphor, because we already have a beam of truth in ourselves. This self-recognition is what gives art, as I mentioned above, its *ethical* value; what allows art to draw out from us a greater sense of "the truth that we are".[340] There is truth in art because there is, first of all, *truth in us*. Gadamer writes to this dialectic as follows:

---

[338] Jean Paul Richter, cited by Ralph Waldo Emerson in *Essays* (London: Everyman's Library, 1906), p. 104. I have here changed the first person singular to the first person plural.

[339] "Imitation and representation are not merely a second version, a copy, but a recognition of the essence". In Gadamer, *TM*, p. 103.

[340] Cf. Gadamer, *PH*, p. 16. On the connection between ethics and self-understanding, see Joanna Hodge, *Heidegger and Ethics* (London: Routledge, 1995); and my review of the same, entitled, "Let Being Be", in *The Times Literary Supplement*, 16 February (1996): 13. My present work on Gadamer, *The Truth That We Are: Gadamer and the Ethics of Transformation*, follows up on this connection in greater depth.

> What one experiences in a work of art and what one is directed
> toward is...how true it is, i.e. to what extent one *knows and
> recognises something and oneself*. But we do not understand
> what recognition is in its deepest sense if we only see that
> something that we know already is known again, i.e. that what
> is familiar is recognised again. The joy of recognition is rather
> that *more* becomes known than is already known.   In
> recognition what we know emerges, as if by illumination,
> from all the contingency and variability of circumstances that
> condition it, *and is grasped in its essence.*[341]

For Gadamer, "recognising" the truthful in art is the subject-
initiated task of grasping the familiar in its genuine essence, removed
from all contingencies, crystallised out of the variety of its historical
relationships, and thereby rendered free to the subjective, imaginative
consciousness "in all the heightened truth of its being". It is not just a
matter of knowing something *again*, but of knowing something
more, and that something more is *ourselves*. From deep inside us
comes a feeling of onto-existential connection that grounds the
experience of recognition, that enables us to direct our attention "to
what extent we know and recognise something and ourselves". Nor
is this act a mere rearranging and polishing of dust-ridden cerebral
shelves: Gadamer describes the experience of this process, as his
fellow Prussian Nietzsche had done before him, as one of "joy"
[*Freude*].[342]

Newman too speaks of a kind of "joy" we feel in "recognising"
something as truthful. The "mark of certitude" he writes is a "feeling
of satisfaction and self-gratulation, of intellectual security arising out
of a sense of success, attainment, possession, finality..."[343]
Moreover, this feeling of repose in the knowing self is not a feeling
achieved *en route*, but rather is the end product of the complex

---

[341] Gadamer, *TM*, p. 102. Italics added.

[342] Among many other references, see Nietzsche, *Thus Spoke Zarathustra*, III, 19; in *The
Portable Nietzsche*, W Kaufmann, ed. and trans. (New York: Viking Portable Library, 1968), pp.
320-21.

[343] Cited in Bernard M G Reardon, *From Coleridge to Gore* (London: Longman Group Ltd., 1971),
p. 138.

knowing act, the *consciousness* of possessing knowledge.[344] It is the satisfaction, to usurp Polanyi's famous phrase, of *"knowing that I know"*. Newman does *not* indicate, however, that the feeling of contentment obtained by the knowing experience is anywhere connected to a deepening of *self*-knowledge. We have seen him speak of concrete experience and conviction as forestructuring the knowing process, and as thus essential to knowing anything at all. But he is far too English—which is to say, and in contrast to the German mind, far too reserved to placard his private holdings—to assume that in knowing something in and through our personal forestructures we might come to know something of ourselves as well.

This comparison raises again the *questio juris*. Given that my assents to objective things, and to assertions about such things, are both forestructured and self-projective, does my feeling convinced of what I believe to be true, as *per* Gadamer's "joy" or Newman's "feeling of satisfaction", provide reason enough not only for the sanction of my own private acts of illation, but also for others to accept those acts as valid, and thus deserving of replication? On what grounds, in other words, does my self-satisfied conquest of knowledge, or my joyful enhancement of self-understanding, stretch itself to universal proportions?

We have seen Gadamer address this question, and noted his solution to be less than satisfactory. It is a question Newman asked as well—"Is there any *criterion* of the accuracy of an inference, such as may be our warrant that certitude is rightly elicited in favour of the proposition inferred, since the warrant [of our illative sense]...cannot be scientific?"[345]—but will his answer be any better? In my reading it is not; and if anything, it is *less* satisfactory than Gadamer's. Newman tells us that there *is* such a criterion, and in theory, like Gadamer, its locus is internal. For certitude admits of its own form of

---

[344] Newman, *GA* p. 134.
[345] Newman, *GA*, p. 134. Emphasis is Newman's.

"indefectibility", which can be demonstrated by the following argument. When one loses one's certitude on an otherwise arguable conviction—when one ceases to believe in God, say—it is sufficient proof that one was never *really* certain of it to begin with; that one's illative sense never *really* gave its full assent from the start, however vociferously it had been held. "Certitude", claims Newman, "ought to stand all trials, or it is not certitude".[346] Once the assent of the illative sense is given, therefore, it is "immutable". One may change one's mind on something, but this in no way proves the truth or falsity of one's first conviction; nor, it follows, the truthfulness of one's subsequent convictions; only that one never possessed the sanction of the illative sense upon it in the first place. Here one wishes Newman had followed up, with his otherwise insightful psychological acumen, the possible links between a "loss of certitude" and his more characteristic, and certainly more thoroughly argued, doctrine of "obedience to the laws of [one's] own nature"; which laws, Newman tells us, change with changing circumstances.[347] For I think there lies in Newman's notions of "self-sufficiency", and the conscience-driven striving after authenticity in one's personal assents, the groundwork for a proto-Gadamerian notion of self-recognition and reflective self-understanding in relation to "the other".

But as it stands, Newman's reasoning is circular, and thus self-defeating. To his credit, Newman recognises his own unsubtlety, yet unfortunately fails to offer any real alternative solution. Instead, he insists—as we have seen him insist previously on a similar issue—that if in matters of faith and moral conduct we are faced with a multiplicity of competing options, and find our illative sense hesitant to render final judgment on any one of them; if in the ebb and flood of changing public mores we find our former assents challenged and unsettled, it is in our best interest to submit ourselves without reserve to the authority of the Roman Catholic church, which alone possesses

---

[346] Newman, *GA*, p. 278.
[347] Newman, *GA*, pp. 272-81.

the ultimate guarantee of veracity. This ultimate submission to a higher, non-rational—in the sense that it is "divine"—authority is a move Newman makes repeatedly, as we have seen; and when taken on its own terms it is not incoherent. But it goes without saying that it also shuts off all further discussion on the matter; and thus, in Gadamerian terms, all further conversation around what is actually experienced and understood.

This should not abrogate altogether Newman's *functional* description of the illative sense as covering those tacit and often unspecifiable processes of inference that govern our judgments. As he well observes, personal judgment plays an important role in the beginning, middle and end of all verbal discussion and inquiry. Where Newman goes wrong, in my opinion—and no doubt in Gadamer's as well were he to have contributed one—is in maintaining that the illative sense is *nothing other than* a personal gift or acquisition, and that it therefore supplies "no common measure between mind and mind". Newman rightly stresses that for reasons of its connectedness to "the whole of one's being", individuals are not able to articulate the reasons lying behind their acts of convictional judgment. But because he does not acknowledge a prior alliance of the "whole" self to the *full* spectrum of temporal-regional historicity, to the *entire* socio-cultural network of human contextuality, and instead restricts it to a single, specified sphere within that totality, Newman fails as a hermeneutic seer. Inasmuch as he divorces human wholeness and authenticity from the wholeness of human civilisation, and places it instead only in the Roman Catholic church, he bars his epistemology from participation in the broader conversation governed by those more general forms of human collective that Gadamer has set as guarantors of universal validity: namely, "tradition" and the *sensus communis*. As we have seen with Gadamer, however problematic tradition may be in its availability to critique, it nevertheless transcends the workings of the individual mind in such a way as to provide a corrective to self-serving interpretations.

In other words, Gadamer holds that if what I believe to be true happens to conflict with what the vast majority of people take to be the case, then it is incumbent upon me to reconsider the grounds of my belief. Newman's position appears, by contrast, to be close to fanaticism. His otherwise healthy preoccupation with the free-wheeling mental states of the individual leads his search not to the open-ended, on-going horizon of *human conversation*, but to the more cloistered embrace of *ecclesiastical authoritarianism*. Is this, however, the only answer to a subject-oriented epistemology of religious knowledge? Is there not some way to assuage the gods of universal validity without kowtowing to those of totalitarian dogmatism? In the following two parts, I want to address this question: first, by examining in greater detail Newman's argument for an infallible source of inferences; and secondly, by proposing an alternative solution.

PART THREE:

Newman and The Problem of Authority

> *On the day when it means something to talk about human limits,*
> *then we shall be faced with the problem of God. But not before;*
> *not before we have lived man's possibilities through to the end.*

Albert Camus, *Notebooks*

In chapter two of his *Essay on Development*, Newman sets out a Butler-esque argument in favour of the historical development of Christian doctrine. Since Christian revelation is itself a rich and complex reality, he argues, and since the human capacity to grasp its subtle nuances is limited, it is the most probable assumption that the identification of the whole of revelation in its various aspects will take time; hence *development* is "to be expected". Newman does not stop there, however. For in order to establish which developments of the original idea are legitimate and which are not, it is likely to expect there to be as well an "infallible organ" of discernment, divinely inspired and thus equipped to distinguish authentic developments from inauthentic:

> If Christianity be a social religion, as it certainly is, and if it be based on certain ideas acknowledged as divine...and if these ideas have various aspects, and make distinct impressions on different minds, and issue in consequence in a multiplicity of

there to be as well an "infallible organ" of discernment, divinely inspired and thus equipped to distinguish authentic developments from inauthentic:

> If Christianity be a social religion, as it certainly is, and if it be based on certain ideas acknowledged as divine...and if these ideas have various aspects, and make distinct impressions on different minds, and issue in consequence in a multiplicity of developments, true, or false, or mixed, as has been shown, what influence will suffice to meet and to do justice to these conflicting conditions, but a supreme authority ruling and reconciling individual judgments by a divine right and a recognised wisdom?...If Christianity is both social and dogmatic, and intended for all ages, it must humanly speaking have an infallible expounder.[348]

Finding a way to bridge the chasm caused by his realisation that Christianity is "both social and dogmatic" is at the heart of Newman's theological work. His life-long search for a way to integrate his historian's mind with his theologian's heart brought him, time and time again, to formulate a theory that embraces, at once, the historical contingency that relativises, and the theological development that expands, the "truth" of the original deposit of Christian faith. He found that bridge in the Roman Catholic doctrine of the magisterium, with its infallible hermeneutical and articulative capacities. I want now to analyse this discovery in greater depth.

AUTHORITY DEFINED

Newman begins his defence of an infallible magisterium by citing the French historian Guizot who writes: "A religion has no sooner arisen in the human mind than a religious society appears; and immediately a religious society is formed, it produces a

---

[348] Newman, *DD*, II. ii. 13.

government".[349] Newman describes this development of positive institutional formation in the *Essay on Development* as "ethical" (in the 1845 version, "moral"), i.e. not only is an external government inevitable but also "desirable" and "appropriate" and not "a matter for strictly logical inference".[350] It is both antecedently probable that such a development will take place, and that it will be authorised by the sanction of God: "the social principle...gives a divine sanction to society and to civil government".[351]

He then moves from this level of generalisation to justify his more particular claim for the divinely decreed teaching authority of the Roman Catholic Church. A cluster of arguments is brought forward to show that "an infallible authority" is "antecedently probable", of which the most important is that divine revelation needs to be interpreted properly at every stage in history, and in such a way that it becomes accessible to the individual: "The very idea of revelation implies a present informant and guide, and that an infallible one; not a mere abstract declaration of truths unknown before to man...but a message and a lesson speaking to this man or that".[352]

This argument, says Newman, is merely "common sense", and is "forced upon us" by such "analogical considerations" as that creation itself cries out for a continual form of government, and that individual people, ever in need of counsel, each possess a "conscience" that supplyies them with an "inward guide" for their ethical decision-making.[353] In other words, if Nature and the human self both need and submit themselves to established hierarchies, how much more ought those who seek God through religious belief?

Demonstration of the need for hierarchy does not necessarily entail the need for a *divine* hierarchy, of course. But if Newman's argument from analogy seems too rhetorical and self-serving to be

---

[349] From Guizot, *European Civilization*, lecture V; cited in Newman, *DD*, I. ii. 8.
[350] Newman, *DD*, I. ii. 6.
[351] Newman, *DD*, I. ii. 7.
[352] Newman, *DD*, II. ii. 12.
[353] Newman, *DD*, II. ii. 10.

persuasive, its general drift at least is abundantly cogent: because we find in history a variety of religious developments, it must be assumed that,

a) some of those developments are true to the original "revelation" or "deposit of faith", and some are not. This being the case, there is

b) a *need* for some criteria of judgment. This need then becomes

c) the ground for our anticipating some form of governing criteria. However, government cannot exist without a political body, so it is reasonable to expect to find

d) an authoritative body that espouses the needed criteria. But government cannot function without a head, so

e) we expect to find, in addition to an institutional hierarchy, a single locus of authoritative power ruling that body. And all this we find readily enough in the Roman Catholic Pope and his episcopate.[354]

The form in which I have worded Newman's argument here is somewhat misleading, however. Newman's fundamental concern, at least in the *Essay on Development*, is less straightforwardly positive: it is rather to "remove a general preliminary objection against Romanism",[355] namely that the existing doctrine and practice of the Roman church is a "corruption".[356] Yet it seems to me, at least, the result is the same. One cannot assent to Newman's argument in favour of a truthful development of the original Christian faith without at the same time giving the nod to the "fact" that the sole authoritative judging facility in decisions of religious knowledge rests in the Roman Church. As Newman puts it in the *Grammer*, "The word of the Church is the word of revelation...the infallible oracle of truth".[357] And at the heart of the Church's authority, he adds

---

[354] Cf. Newman, *DD*, IV. iii. 8; II. iii. 2; VI. ii. 13.

[355] William Cunningham, "Newman on Development", *North British Review*, V (1846): 432.

[356] Newman, *DD*, IV. iii. 7. Cf. Nicholas Lash, *Newman on Development*, pp. 40-41.

[357] Newman, *GA*, p. 131.

elsewhere, is the Pope:

> The voice of Peter is now, as it ever has been, a real authority, infallible when it teaches, prosperous when it commands, ever taking the lead wisely and distinctly in its own province, adding certainty to what is probable, and persuasion to what is certain.[358]

This is not to say that Newman did not maintain a certain Anglican reserve about papal infallibility, even as a cardinal. Having stated the foregoing, it should also be mentioned that if taken as a whole, Newman's attitude toward infallibility, and in general toward the primacy of the Catholic Church, is at best mixed.[359] After all, he claimed to have believed to the end in the freedom of individual conscience, that "divine law" which resides in every human soul.[360] In his much-debated *Letter to the Duke of Norfolk*, Newman in effect formulates the rule, affirmed at Vatican II,[361] that one should disobey *any* authority, papal or otherwise, which one judges by the light of one's conscience to be contrary to morality:[362]

> I should look to see what theologians could do for me, what the Bishops and clergy around me, what my confessor; what friends whom I have revered: and if, after all, I could not take their view of the matter, then I must rule myself by my own judgment and my own conscience".[363]

---

[358] From a sermon entitled "Cathedra Sempiterna" that Newman preached as a Roman Catholic in 1856, and reprinted in S Jaki, ed., *Newman Today*, p. 221.

[359] On the issue of papal infallibility, see Newman's *Letter to the Duke of Norfolk*, where he writes, "Hence, I have never been able to see myself that the ultimate decision rests with any but the general Catholic intelligence"; cited in I Ker, *John Henry Newman*, p. 681. And on a more general topic, see LD, XXV. 71, where Newman states: "It does not follow that because there is no Church but one...that therefore no one can be saved without the intervention of that one Church".

[360] Cf. Ker and Hill, eds., *Newman After a Hundred Years*, p. 169.

[361] Cf. *Guadium et Spes*, "Pastoral Constitution on the Church in the Modern World" (1965), paragraph 16. "In the depths of conscience, man discerns a law which he does not dictate to himself but which he ought to obey...for man has in his heart a law written by God..." Cf. also, P Delhaye, *The Christian Conscience*, C U Quinn trans. (New York: 1968), esp. ch. 3.

[362] At least this is how John Finnis reads Newman; cf. J. Finnis, "Conscience in the *Letter to the Duke of Norfolk*"; in Ker and Hill, *Newman After a Hundred Years*, pp. 401-18.

[363] Newman, *Letter to the Duke of Norfolk*, pp. 243-44.

In addition, there are ways to explain Newman's retreat into authoritarianism, and the role it plays in his epistemology, which may help us understand his theory from a more *hermeneutical*, which is to say, less straightforwardly literal, perspective. John Coulson, for example, tells us that Newman's high view of ecclesiastical authority is expressive not of his fear of human freedom, as Gadamer might have supposed,[364] but of his aesthetic and imaginative sensitivity to the nature of human finitude in light of the *structure* of Christian revelation. Revelation, writes Newman, is of the structure of "mystery" and of "a doctrine *lying hid* in language".[365] It relies on the accumulation of probabilities rather than sheer logic; it houses only "detached and incomplete truths". Hence, the reason we must hold to a propositional revelation and its institutional guarantor is that, apart from doctrines and verbal formulations, "revelation does not exist, there being nothing else given us by which to ascertain or enter into it".[366] However whole-heartedly we may assent to the mysterious "language" of scripture and of our own religious experiences, the question remains—what are we to believe? Our acceptance of an infallible authority is thus, at least in Coulson's reading of Newman, really an acceptance of something more along the lines of "a literary culture";[367] i.e. we accept as trustworthy the statements of those religious authorities whose role it is to be the *conservatoire* of the traditions handed on by the community of faith, and which in turn give shape to what we ultimately believe about God.

Of course, traditions are shaped and sometimes *distorted* by the various acts associated with the historically conditioned "handing-

---

[364] Cf. Gadamer, *TM*, pp. 211f. Gadamer writes, "The human mind, seeking protection and certainty, sets against this 'frightful countenance' [of its own freedom] the scientifically developed capacity of understanding. It is supposed to reveal life in its social, historical reality in so far that, despite the ultimate incomprehensibility of life, knowledge imparts protection and certainty".

[365] Newman, *ECH*, vol. 1, 41-2. Emphasis is Newman's.

[366] Newman, *ECH*, p. 47.

[367] John Coulson, *Religion and Imagination*, p. 75.

on" process. This is the argument of Jürgen Habermas I mentioned above; namely, that human discourse cannot but be skewed by the very nature of its being human. Still, in Coulson's reading, Newman holds that the believer has every right to look to its ecclesiastical authorities with a sense of believing trust; they are after all the "connoisseurs"[368] of practical faith; they have—ideally speaking—submitted themselves to the full requirements of the tradition; lived out its various strictures; are familiar with its language, grammar and "word-games"; and by this very expertise embody the tradition in their own persons. Because of their participation in these traditive forces of faith development and *Bildung*, ecclesiastical authorities keep the fullness of the Christian faith "alive" and accessible to the believer-in-the-world who otherwise has neither the time nor the incentive for such a level of commitment.

I would want to add to Coulson's remarks, however, that the kind of authority which *ought to* attend the valuation of religious beliefs must at all points remain sensitive to the *personal* nature of such beliefs. As Vico has shown, the more precious a piece of knowledge, the more personal its acquisition.[369] Religious beliefs are perhaps the most precious bits of knowledge we possess. According to John Bowker in *The Sense of God*, we humans have "scanned the limitations that surround us" and searched for "a way through", especially a "way through death". In so doing, we have developed religious beliefs and doctrines as a kind of "route-finding activity"; i.e. in order to "provide the means through which the significance of [our] actions and lives can be identified".[370] Acceptance of or "assent" toward religious doctrines is thus a form of what Polanyi has called "convictional knowing", a phrase that parallels what Newman

---

[368] The phase is Michael Polanyi's, from *Personal Knowledge*, pp. 54-55.

[369] Vico defines his famous *verum-factum* principle as the dictum: we can only know fully what we have created; hence the more intimate our knowledge, the more personally involved with it we must be. Cf. Donald Phillip Verene, *Vico's Science of Imagination* (Ithaca: Cornell University Press, 1981), pp. 36-64; and Andrew Louth, *Discerning the Mystery* (Oxford: Clarendon Press, 1983), pp. 18f.

[370] John Bowker, *The Sense of God* (Oxford: Clarendon Press, 1973), pp. 63-64.

termed "real", as opposed to "notional", Christian knowledge.[371]
Convictional knowing implies an "indwelling"[372] of, i.e. a personally
motivated penetration into, what is known. It is this personal
involvement that gives religious knowledge its autonomy; there is a
self-authenticating aesthetic about it that is violated by the objective
imposition of certitude from some extra- or non-personal source.

ouch!

"Doctrine is an activity", writes Nicholas Lash, "...an aspect of
pedagogy".[373] Authoritative statements of religious knowledge are,
in the etymological sense of *auctoritas*, originative and evocative;
they incite us to much self-reflection and "soul-searching"; but they
are not the last word on what we may expect to find there. This is to
say, they mark a starting point for reflection, but not the end. In
George Lindbeck's terms, doctrines are "second-order propositions",
not "first-order"; meaning that they make "grammatical" and
"regulative" rather than "ontological" truth claims.[374] According to
Lindbeck, doctrines issue in "communally authoritative rules of
discourse, attitude, and action"; and this is "the *only* job that
doctrines do in their role as church teachings".[375] In a similar vein,
Matthew Arnold wrote (over one hundred years before Lindbeck) that
the Church's basic "forms" of religious knowledge, i.e. its dogmas and
creeds, once purged of their "sacerdotalism" can be "retained as
symbolising, with the force and charm of poetry, a few cardinal facts

---

[371] On "convictional knowing", see Loder, *The Transforming Moment,* chs. IV and V; and on
Newman's distinction between the "notional" and the "real", see *GA,* ch. IV; and H H Price,
Belief, ch. II. 5.

[372] "Indwelling" is a term that was used first by Vico, then by Wilhelm Dilthey and Gadamer as
a protest against the Enlightenment's ideals of objectivity and detachment. It stems from the
theory that of the things of human culture—art, history, literature—we have an intuitive,
cognitive connection; whereas the things of nature are more or less opaque. Interpretation is thus
a "process of imaginative amplification" of this fundamental "connaturality of identity". See,
Isaiah Berlin, *Against the Current* (London: 1980), pp. 80-110; Andrew Louth, *Discerning the
Mystery,* pp. 17-44; Vico, *The New Science,* I. ii. 11-12 and I. iii; H A Hodges, *Wilhelm
Dilthey: An Introduction,* (London: 1944), pp. 14-17.

[373] Nicholas Lash, *Easter in Ordinary* (London: SCM Press, 1988), p. 258.

[374] George Lindbeck, *The Nature of Doctrine* (Philadelphia: Westminster Press, 1984), p. 80. On
the application of "first-order" and "second-order" to the Patristic doctrine of the *homoousios,*
see Bernhard Lonergan, "The Dehellinization of Dogma", in *Second Collection,* W Ryan and B
Tyrrell, eds. (Philadelphia: Westminster Press, 1974).

[375] George Lindbeck, *The Nature of Doctrine,* pp. 18-19.

and ideas, simple indeed, but indispensable and inexhaustible, and on which our race could lay hold only by materialising them".[376]

I take Arnold's remark to be especially telling. There is a grammatical "force" to religious doctrine, if only rarely a "charm", that mimics the aesthetic experience one has in one's encounter with poetry. Both poetry and religious dogma attain their success not when they "lull and satisfy us, but when they astonish and fire us with new endeavours after the unattainable";[377] and they only do so, *ala* Lash and Arnold, when they are in some way "performed" or "materialised", i.e. indwellt and tested for what in them can be assented to, under the light of conscience, as true.[378] This is not to say that doctrinal statements are *merely* poetic. But the *development* of doctrine, as Newman conceives it, is analogous to the kind of growth in consciousness great poets have always envisaged. "Revealed religion should be especially poetical", writes Newman, for "...it brings us into a new world".[379] When one takes time to "perform" the mysteries of religion; when one devotes both meditative and *practical* attention to religious truth-claims, one may discover, on analogy with the aesthetic experience of poetry, that some aspect of them will "click into place", enabling us to understand in a new way the grander mystery of the whole.[380] Since present consciousness is

---

[376] Matthew Arnold, "Irish Catholicism and British Liberalism" in *Mixed Essays*, (London: 1880), pp. 118-21.

[377] Ralph Waldo Emerson, *Essays*, p. 104.

[378] On the "performance" of truth, see Gadamer, *TM*, pp. 104f and 121f; and Nicholas Lash, "Performing the Scriptures", in *Theology on the Way to Emmaus* (London: SCM Press, 1986), ch. 3.

[379] Newman, *ECH*, vol. 1, p. 23.

[380] Edward Bullough writes, "When a work of art is successfully apprehended...the new aesthetic object which is actualised to awareness is perceived with more lucidity, as if a caul had been removed from in front of it. It is sharper and more vivid in detail as if it had been removed from the periphery to the focus of vision and it acquires a structure by which it is compacted into a unified configuration"; in *Aesthetics: Lectures and Essays* (London: Bowes and Bowes, 1957) p. 174.

Of modern religious writers, Simone Weil has probably been most explicit about the powers of what she calls "attention". Though she does not explicitly draw the parallel with aesthetic perception, her account of religious attention is wholly consistent with the view I am developing here. See, "Reflections on the Right Use of School Studies with a View to the Love of God", in *Waiting for God*, (New York: G P Putnam, 1951), pp. 105-116.

mutable and relative, however, this "click" will not hold indefinitely. One is thus forever having to readjust one's convictional knowing from one level of commitment to another. Frames of knowledge, useful in former times but now no longer so, must be discarded and replaced by more relevant ones.[381]

Does it follow from my presentation here that we are condemned to theological relativism? No, not necessarily. Although the strained attempts we make at "re-framing" our religious knowledge will always fall short of completeness—here we can recall Newman's asymptotic "polygon" illustration—they nevertheless imply that there is a *something* there to be attained. Logically, to speak as Newman does of "approximation" is to imply the objective existence of what one is trying to approximate. Theological development is thus, in Newman's account, a real growth in understanding, an expansion of horizon, even if full maturity is never reached. In fact, it is this very incompleteness that makes development possible in the first place. As Newman puts it, theology "makes progress" by forever "being...alive to its own fundamental uncertainties".[382]

At the heart of what spurs on this progress is a genuine *trust* in the reality of the original idea. As Coulson writes,

> Because faith, however conceived, is a spontaneous act, and because spontaneity...presupposes trust, without trust there can be no faith. To allow imagination to diffuse and dissipate where there is initially no acceptance of someone or something as trustworthy, is to risk inevitable disintegration and dissociation...probabilities fail to converge into certitude; the leap of faith falls short.[383]

Coulson's description shows imagination to be dependent upon a prior act of trust, which then expresses itself in the believer who strives to complete the "ambiguous" and empirically unverifiable

---

[381] Cf. George Lindbeck, *The Nature of Doctrine*, pp. 85-87.
[382] Newman, *PN*, vol. 1, p. 145.
[383] John Coulson, *Religion and Imagination*, p. 76.

knowledge of God through the experimental working-out of his or her beliefs in the day to day "performance" of them.[384] In Gadamerian terms, the believer "anticipates" a knowledge of God in and through the act of believing that there is a God who wills to be known; that God's mode of Being is as a Being that gives of itself to human knowledge. In Newmanian terms, one trustingly fills in the blank spaces between the human and the divine by means of illation, imagination and faith.

But, as Gadamer's work has at least theoretically demonstrated, and Newman's work more or less ignored, such completion of religious knowledge is inextricably *social*: religious belief-acts and knowledge cohere within communities that share common frameworks of interpretation, common languages and traditions— what Newman calls "polities".[385] And here lies the real crux of the problem of authority. As we have seen, the verbal and symbolic character of faith passed on by tradition is a "many-faced challenge"[386] that never reaches full term. It never reaches full term because it is social and historical: its "many faces" reflect the many grammars, vocabularies and semantic referencings of its various historical contributors, each adding to the whole, and each addition a transforming "fusion of horizons". Faith-language is much more than a mere set of words "thrown out" at what it can never fully encompass; it is also a fully human face expressing by its wrinkles and spots the very various human epochs that lie behind it. "Language is the house of Being", declares Heidegger, and "in its home man dwells".[387] Religious language, by extension, is only as authoritative as the people who choose to dwell in its home. Although religious

---

[384] Newman writes, "By trying we make proof; by doing we come to know" (*PPS*, viii, p. 113), and "That a thing is true, is no reason that it should be said, but that it should be done" (*PPS*, v, p. 45).

[385] Cf. John Coulson, *Religion and Imagination*, p. 78.

[386] John Coulson, *Newman and the Common Tradition* (Oxford: Clarendon Press, 1970), p. 76.

[387] Martin Heidegger, "Letter on Humanism", in *Basic Writings*, D Krell, ed. (London: Routledge, 1977), p. 217.

authorities—popes, priests, theologians—assert their right to determine the grammar of religious language, it is in fact the mass of believers themselves, whether wittingly so or not, who continually rearrange its semantics, who alter its facade, giving it always a more human appearance. Hence while religious authorities might attempt to offer "infallible" guidance as to our interpretations, it is only in our own characteristic ways of dwelling within the larger frame of religious language that they come to be verified and valued. And human dwelling is never as black and white as the propositions which presume guide it.

well.. this isn't really congruit w/ch.

AUTHORITY, ART AND TRADITION RE-DEFINED

The message of Michaelangelo's *Last Judgment*,[388] though backed by institutional certification (it covers a wall of the Sistine), is hardly what anyone would call dogmatic. It is far too duplicitous a work. Is Christ's arm raised in blessing or judgment? Why his muscular, satyric appearance, his subtle Dionysian smirk? And why does the mouth of Hell stand gaping over the high altar of the Pope's chapel? The very mark of the *Last Judgment*'s genius, i.e. its polysemy, seems thus to undermine its religious utility as a guiding norm for faith and practice. To view the painting in person is to set in motion a flurry of semantic juxtapositions that repel any sort of propositional integration. Mediated by the human imagination, Michaelangelo's masterpiece *metaphorically* constructs new approaches to reality: by counterpositioning opposing concepts—blessing and curse, revelry and suffering, God's earthly kingdom and Satan's subterrestrial one—it opens up new possibilities for viewing the world, new possibilities for being-in-the-world. This is what is meant by art's "authority", its *auctoritas*: its very irresolution and ambiguity tend to push reason into new territory, encouraging the

---

[388] Vatican City, Sistine Chapel: 1541.

horizon of one's affections to expand.

I want here to suggest that religion, like art, is also about the business of constructing new avenues into the realities hidden in our temporal-regional worlds. Religion represents a series of creative, imaginative responses of either individuals or collectives to what is apprehended as the sacred or transcendent aspects of human being-in-the-world.[389] Religion is "a cultural and symbolic system", writes Clifford Geertz, "that tunes human affections to an envisaged cosmic order and projects images of cosmic order onto the plane of human experience".[390] One can say, then, that religion "bodies forth" or incarnates in positive form a whole spectrum of human needs and concerns. Its pedagogical function is to aid us in living well, responsibly and authentically. Religion, in other words, is in the business of orienting human flourishing toward what is good and true. Through its sacred stories, symbols and rituals, religion conveys a sense of what matters most in life by referencing lived experience to that which lies beyond. Like the metaphorical element in Michaelangelo's *Last Judgment*, religion juxtaposes opposing categories of Being—time and eternity, darkness and light, good and evil—so that in the hermeneutical spaces between them we may somehow come to find ourselves at home. Religious metaphors mirror the oppositional tensions in our own lives, and create fields of interpretation wherein those tensions can be resolved in personally significant ways. All of which is to say: religion's authority lies not in its institution or hierarchy, but rather in the faithful experiences of individual believers who have proved, by the test of time, the transformative effectiveness of the religious traditions they have inherited.

I do not discount that it is a desirable thing to have an authoritative body of governors whose representation of the

---

[389] Cf. Joachim Wach, *Types of Religious Experience: Christian and Non-Christian* (Chicago: University of Chicago Press, 1951), pp. 32-33.
[390] Clifford Geertz, "Religion As a Cultural System", in *The Interpretation of Cultures* (New York: Basic Books, 1973), p. 90.

particular traditions it oversees is to some degree faithful and trustworthy; and which can be trusted to search for new, more appropriate interpretations that are yet contiguous with its own historical affirmations. But it is not, *contra* Newman, a thing we can "anticipate" human history to provide. Despite my constant Gadamerian revisions, there still remains about Newman's argument for an *infallible* authority something wholly inconsistent both with his more general epistemology of religious knowledge, and with the sort of hermeneutical consciousness Gadamer espouses. Is it possible to argue so strongly for a religious knowledge based upon first principles, antecedent probabilities and illative judgments; which can only be expressed in provisional, approximate formulae; and which changes over time according to the influences of history, culture and personal taste, while at the same time holding to an infallible source of authority whose locus is an historical institution, i.e. the Roman Catholic Church and its various Popes? Should it not follow from Newman's account of history, ideological development, personal judgment and religious language that the very institution that presumes to be the keeper of the tradition and worthy of our trust is itself subject to the same relativising forces that impinge upon our own private beliefs?

To raise these questions, of course, is to risk an abandonment of Newman—as well as the Catholic church—as a reliable resource for methodological reflection in the study of religious knowledge. I have tried to salvage Newman's theory without relegating it to the annals of either a religious relativism or an extreme dogmatism. But I must conclude that to read Newman *in toto* is to find oneself hanging precariously, perhaps inextricably between the two.

As I see it, the crux of the problem lies with Newman's insistence, outlined above, on tradition as a cumulative but irreversible horizon of ideological interpretations, set down in institutionally certified dogmas, as historical pressures are brought to bear on an idea's very various potential for expression. It is the ambiguous nature of this expressive potentiality that leads Newman into his all-too-convenient argument for interpretative closure, i.e. the "dogmatic principle". But this is only one way of understanding the nature of tradition. According to Gadamer, and by way of reversing the Newmanian priority, the principal dynamic of tradition is "trans-mediation" rather than "trans-mission".[391] Mediation does not imply that one simply passes on an unchanged body of beliefs. It signifies an active process of appropriation in which each historical epoch learns to grasp and make present past beliefs in new and fresh ways, ways that are faithful, not to some idealised event in the past (as *per* Newmanian dogmatics), but to *the fundamental continuity of history itself* as the indefeasible medium encompassing every interpretation. Tradition is such a continuity of "presencings" or mediations through which the present transforms past horizons of understanding, even as the past transforms present ways of understanding.

To demonstrate this, Gadamer uses the illustration of an experience he had when visiting a series of ancient cathedrals in southern Spain. Because their age and rural remoteness prevented them from having electricity, their interiors were lit only by candles and what natural light could filter through the narrow portals of their walls. Accustomed to viewing architectural forms under artificial light, Gadamer exclaimed that this more natural way of seeing was "the only proper way to encounter these mighty citadels of religion".[392] But such an insight, he comments, would have been impossible without the juxtaposition of present ways of living—electric brightness, clarity of vision, switching light on and off at will—with the way things used to be in the past. He adds, of course, that this does not mean we should give up electric lighting in modern churches, for "it is no more possible to do this than to disregard all the other aspects of modern life". But it does illustrate an important point

---

[391] Gadamer, *RB*, pp. 48-49. And compare David Linge's discussion in "Editor's Introduction", *PH*, pp. xviff.
[392] Gadamer, *RB*, p. 49.

on the nature of tradition: for where the past has been allowed to creep into our present experience, it forces a "constant interaction between our aims in the present and the past to which we still belong"; the past's "effective-history" [*Wirkungsgeschichte*]393 forces a hermeneutical encounter that demands both our attention and our appropriation.   All of which is to say that tradition is a dynamic process, full of transformative potential both for our readings of the past and for our understandings of the present.

Unfortunately, Gadamer is better at explaining what he wants to do than doing what he explains.   Warnke, Habermas, Caputo and other critics are right to claim that Gadamer's *practical* view of tradition, as I mentioned above, is an essentially conservative one.394 Ultimately he leaves little ground for critical detachment from and judgment upon the traditions that mediate our cognition.   Yet everything he points to in his more theoretical moments suggests that tradition is really about "openness"; that the narrow-minded exclusivity associated with *traditionalism* has little place in the modern world.   The Spanish cathedrals remind us, in effect, that tradition's mode of being is a *present* openness to the past in the dynamic of "encounter" that works toward, at least potentially if not actually, a fresh revision of our aims and understandings.   To put it in Heideggerian terms, tradition is a "letting-be" [*Gelassen*] of the past "for us as we are now"; not in the sense of passive acceptance, but of an active, critically thinking and evaluating encounter.

This more theoretical understanding of tradition is, as I have tried to show, common both to Gadamer's metaphor of "fusion" and Newman's theory of "development" and religious epistemology. Superficially at least, Gadamer and Newman are alike in wanting to achieve some sense of finality, and are thus alike in getting into trouble with respect to the more historically conscious aspects of their own theories.   Despite his arguments for historical revision and

---

393 Cf. Gadamer, *TM*, pp. 267ff., 305ff., 310, 324ff., 414, and 429ff.
394 Cf. Georgia Warnke, *Gadamer*, ch. 4; and John Caputo, *Radical Hermeneutics* (Bloomington: Indiana University Press, 1987), pp. 96-97, 108-115.

personal modes of judgment, Newman all-too-quickly turns to an infallible ecclesiology; while Gadamer, despite arguing for horizonal transformation, does something similar—albeit in a more qualified way—with his conservative estimate of tradition. If we can conclude that an infallible ecclesiastical authority is, on an hermeneutical analysis, implausible; and if the unquestionable enshrinement of any particular tradition has to be rejected on the same as well as moral grounds, what then are we left with as our source for reliable inferences? It is this question that I want now to address, at least indirectly, in the final section that follows.

PART FOUR:

Toward an Aesthetics of Religious Knowing

> *Everywhere I am bereaved of meeting God in my brother,*
> *because he has shut the his own temple-doors,*
> *and recites fables merely of his brother's,*
> *or his brother's brother's God.*

Ralph Waldo Emerson, "Self-Reliance"

I said at the outset of this book that my main project is to establish some degree of correspondence between Newman's epistemology and Gadamer's reclamation of classical aesthetics. I am satisfied that up to this point this purpose has been accomplished. I think I am right in saying that at major points in each of their respective "systems"—and I use the term loosely—there is a great degree of similarity in the way the two men approach the problem of knowledge. I would even add that, allowing for differences in vocabulary, in certain instances— "first principles", for example, or on the notion of "anticipation"—the two writers approach a near total agreement. We have seen as well, although less happily, that the Newmanian and Gadamerian systems each possess a similar range of internal contradictions, and that each sets about to resolve those contradictions, then fails to resolve them, in similar ways. There is, of course, a fundamental distinction between Newman's religious and empiricist frame of thinking, and Gadamer's existential, hermeneutical approach, and which I have endeavoured to describe. Nevertheless, I maintain that the degree of correspondence is strikingly positive, as I hope the foregoing has demonstrated, and thus invites commentary on just how this correspondence might venture forth into the study of religion proper.

It has in no way been my intent up to this point to press my Newman-Gadamer correspondence in the direction of any sort of detached prescription. Yet enough questions about relativism and subjectivity have been raised in the course of this discussion, some answered and some merely posed, that it seems best by way of a concluding statement to pressure these two thinkers into offering a solution. The problem that lays before me now is the problem of religious knowledge. I will suggest by the following, in light of what we have learned from Newman and Gadamer, that for all its forced epistemological bravado, and for all its historically conditioned ambiguity, human reason still desires to know something of God; and desires that its knowledge of God be trustworthy and true. It has been my suggestion all along, however, that a Newman-Gadamer synthesis leaves us without recourse to any sort of divinely inspired final word on all other final words about God; that the hope for an infallible source of reliable inferences about the divine nature, whether institutional or textual, will forever go unmet. In light of these restrictions, then, I would like to propose an alternative model. In the following, I am offering a model of religious knowledge in three various aspects, and of the three human modes of knowing that attend these aspects; a model that seems to me to resolve the tension between the subjectivity of knowledge Newman and Gadamer both so strongly support, and at the same time the unquenchable human desire, and desparate need, for objectivity. My model suggests that religious knowledge, our knowledge of God, is rightly conceived, and most effectively appropriated, when it is placed under one or other of three categories: the symbolic, the imaginative and the experiential.

SYMBOLIC KNOWING

I have been concerned throughout this study with religious knowledge: the ways by which it is attained and the problems attendant with those ways. In his *Critique of Judgment*, Kant states that "all our knowledge of God is symbolic".[395] To think otherwise, warns Kant, would not only be to "fall into anthropomorphism", but it would also be to mistake the nature of knowledge itself. For knowledge, asserts Kant, must necessarily be a matter of applying intellectual concepts to the materials afforded us through the senses; and we can have no real sense-experience of God.

Kant has a further distinction to make.[396] When we perceive an object as *beautiful*, we perceive its form or finality as conforming to certain aesthetic laws; i.e. laws of symmetry, harmony, order, and so on. This is even true in cases where the form has to be supplied by the imagination, such as our experience of spiritual beauty. In such a case, it is the imagination that brings the object under the aesthetic laws, however indeterminate our "perception" may be. Our perception of "the beautiful", in other words, is something we can talk about; something that can be put into universal terms.

When we perceive an object as *sublime*, however, things are different. Such objects are "ill-adapted to our faculty of presentation"; they are, says Kant vividly, "an *outrage* on the imagination". Which is to say, they are inexpressible; they render the articulative faculties mute. Yet far from being dismissed as mere aberrations, they are to be "judged", says Kant, "all the more sublime on that account".[397] Such objects evoke a "feeling of the sublime" that contravenes our powers of judgment; we experience a "something there", perhaps, but are powerless to conceive of what it is. But the

---

[395] Cited in Mary Warnock, "Religious Imagination", in James Mackey, ed., *Religious Imagination* (Edinburgh: University Press, 1986), p. 144.
[396] Cf. Paul Crowther, *The Kantian Sublime*, p. 15.
[397] Paul Crowther, *The Kantian Sublime*, pp. 144-45. Italics added.

"it" of "whatever it is" is no less real for its non-conceptuality. Nor is the feeling of the sublime, note, any less an *imaginative* action. Kant is merely making a *functional* distinction here: judgment of the sublime is regulative rather than constitutive.

The point is this: in our apprehension of beauty, understanding and imagination work together in such a way that we see a pattern arising, something we can describe in words—"beautiful", "harmonious", "symmetrical", etc. But of "the sublime" we cannot have any "clear and distinct" idea or image. There is no form to be grasped, no pattern to be adduced. This is perhaps why we often say the sublime leaves us "speechless". If we speak about the sublime at all, we are forced to use a less conventional system of reference.

Referencing sublime objects, therefore, must be done by means of symbols. When we with our imaginations perceive in nature, art or music something we would call "sublime"—the great ideals, for example: God, Freedom or Immortality—what we have done is to move beyond the sensible range of descriptive terms. We have taken up a symbol. In this case, a symbol takes the place of the sensible thing; it is a stand-in for what cannot be otherwise under-stood.

Thus it is natural for Kant to say that all our knowledge of God is symbolic. And for the most part, in light of my Newman-Gadamer synthesis, I agree. There are, of course, certain non-symbolic, true statements to be made about God: that "God is other than the world", or that "God is greater than all I can imagine God to be". But these propositions are of a more apophatic order; they give us knowledge about what God is *not*, not what God *is*. To understand them is to reproduce in one's mind the logical reasoning which led to their position—i.e. God is by definition such and such, and therefore cannot be such and such, etc—all of which remains at the level of grammar and semantics. By "symbolic", on the other hand, I have in mind a series of more *existential* claims, such as "God is love" or "God is three persons in unity". As symbols, these stand in for the *positive* human intuition that the notions of love and relationality in some way represent the divine being. They are also, by the same line of reasoning, notions that symbolise human being. Symbolic understanding, in other words, as opposed to logical or semantical analysis, displays a rationality of imaginative reflection and projection; a rationality that takes human self-understanding seriously as a first principle; and as such it coördinates well, I want to suggest, with the sort of epistemology espoused by both Newman and Gadamer.[398]

Positive knowledge of God, therefore, involves working through symbols. This is done when the things of our ordinary world—i.e. the objects of sense experience—are understood as signifying something beyond themselves; are read *sub specie aeternitatis*; when intuition and feeling see through temporal realities to the infinite horizon that surrounds them, and in turn gives them their true significance. "A symbol", writes Gadamer, "is the coincidence of sensible appearance and supra-sensible meaning".[399] This is not far from the theory of nature we saw espoused by Joseph Bulter, and taken up by Newman in his "sacramental principle": that natural things can be construed via the imagination as universally, even religiously meaningful. Such a theory fuelled the poetic fires of Keats, Wordsworth and Coleridge, in addition to the epistemology of Newman and the aesthetics of Gadamer. In its essence, the symbolic grasping of the sublime is not an intellectual, but an imaginative, affective response. It is the feeling of love working through imagination:

> ...to fear and love,
> To love as prime and chief, for there fear ends,
> Be this ascribed: to early intercourse,
> In presence of sublime or beautiful forms,
> With the adverse principles of pain and joy... ·
> This spiritual Love acts not nor can exist

---

[398] Newman, influenced here by Alexandrian spirituality, demonstrates his affirmation of the symbolic nature of our knowledge of God in his interpretation of the Athanasian Creed. The "antithetical form of its sentences", he writes, mirror the very "mysteriousness" of God; though a "stumbling block" to many, it "is intended as a check upon our reasonings" lest they "rush on in one direction beyond the truth". Cf. *GA* pp. 117-18.

[399] Gadamer, *TM*, p. 70.

> Without Imagination, which, in truth,
> Is but another name for absolute power
> And clearest insight...[400]

These sentiments of Wordsworth that stress "Love" and "Imagination" as constituents of symbolic knowing, when applied to matters of religion stress the irreducibly *human* character of religious knowledge. It is the human in all her historical temporal-regionality who experiences what can only be expressed symbolically; who performs the expressing; and who interprets those expressions as they are handed on in the trans-mediation of tradition. Love can be fickle, and imagination delusional, but these are the risks we take in affirming the symbolic nature of our religious knowledge.

Symbolic knowing can be expressed in ways other than words. As F W Dillistone reminds us,[401] *people* can be symbols too. Geertz defines the religious symbol as that which synthesises and integrates "the world as lived and the world as imagined" in such a way as to produce and strengthen religious conviction.[402] By this definition, one could say that each of the great religions or religious philosophies has had a central *symbolic* figure whose integration of reality and imagination was of such creative strength and relevance as to inspire religious commitment. Moses, Mohammed, Jesus, Buddha, Socrates: each gained followers, but never—if we are to trust recent historical reconstructions—for the purpose of being worshipped. They were *symbols*, each displaying the right balance between embodying the sublimities of their teaching, and pointing beyond themselves to the transcendent reality of which they taught. In this sense none were absolute incarnations; each stood-in for what they were trying to reveal. But this standing-in-for was never in any case a perfection of

---

[400] Wordsworth, *Prelude* (1805 edition), book XIV, 98.

[401] Cf. F W Dillistone, *The Power of Symbols in Religion and Culture* (New York: Crossroad, 1986), pp. 230-35.

[402] Cf. Clifford Geertz, *Anthropological Approaches to the Study of Religion*, M Banton, ed. (London: Methuen, 1968), p. 28.

understanding, for no earthly form, however symbolic, can circumscribe "the sublime". All of which ensures that as long as religious devotees continue to exist, there will be a very varied set of interpretations of the symbols to which they commit themselves.

The Christian religion centres upon the symbolic figure of Jesus of Nazareth. His teachings and deeds became for his disciples the symbol of God's purpose for all creation, and of God's reconciling activity among people. Jesus became the Christ, symbol of God's intention and love. In Gadamerian terms, Jesus became the Christ through the "effective-historical" power of symbolic knowing: in reflecting imaginatively and affectively upon their experiences of Jesus, his followers came to the conclusion, since developed over time, that he was and is a symbol of God's presence in and concern for creation. This transformation, from Jewish carpenter to central Christian symbol, is a *hermeneutical* occurance. As such, it is subject to the sort of revision and ontological heightening we have seen theorised in certain aspects of Newman's work on dogmatic development, and in Gadamer's hermeneutical analysis of aesthetic representation. Only one must be careful, in ascribing this connection, to avoid their same pitfalls.[403]

IMAGINATIVE KNOWING

My reading here of Kant and Wordsworth suggests that it is the imagination, prompted by love, that works through symbols to achieve what we can recognise of sublime realities. The loss of imagination, therefore, is the loss of the ability to see *through* objects in the natural world to the universal realities they may suggest; or if that seems too strong a statement, then the loss of the *experience*, common to all who read nature *sub specie aeternitatis* (poets,

---

[403] For a more detailed description of the transformation of the Christ tradition, and one that refers explicitly to both Gadamer and Newman, see John Macquarrie, *Jesus Christ in Modern Thought* (London: SCM Press, 1990), pp. 12f.

mystics, philosophers, artists), that there must be "something more" to reality than what we perceive with our senses. Without the hermeneutical aid of imagination, each thing simply is what it is and nothing further. There is no "sublime" by which things may be referenced in a way that makes them "more" than what were. And with the loss of an imaginative taste for the sublime, it goes without saying, comes the loss of religious sensibility.[404] For what can we know of God if the images of the material world are all that exist for us?

Not only is imagination a faculty that, via symbols, establishes cognitive contact with God—the experience of Blake's "seeing eternity in a grain of sand", e.g.—but in addition to the Kantian "feeling of the sublime", imagination has the potential to facillitate in us a certain sensation of *ecstasy*, Proust's, "le joie", Milton's "enormous bliss", Nietzsche's "feeling of divinity". Like Thoreau, the *sensation* an active imagination affords, especially one regularly turned to "sublime" things, is that of being "grandly related", of "belonging to the universe".[405]

In the twelfth volume of his masterpiece *Remembrance of Things Past*, Marcel Proust describes the experience of a time when he felt unusually dejected, lacking all joy and creative freedom. While waiting at the door of a friend's home, the narrator pauses to reflect on his state of depression. As the door opens, he takes a step back, accidentally stumbles, and to regain his balance inadvertently places his feet over a pair of uneven paving stones. But much to his surprise, at the feeling of the uneven stones he is filled not with fear or embarrassment, but with "an amazing delight". Moreover, he knows immediately that he has experienced this same sensation of "delight" somewhere else, at some time in the past. With what memory is such

---

[404] Coleridge writes of this as the greatest and most irreparable loss. In his *Dejection: an Ode*, he describes what happens when he can look at the stars and moon and "see, not feel, how beautiful they are". "I may not hope", he continues, "from outward forms to win / The passion and the life, whose fountains are within".

[405] Cited in Willa Muir, *Belonging* (London: Hogarth Press, 1968), p. 23.

a feeling associated, he asks himself? To what distant place and time is this present sensation connected? It was then that he recalls a similar pair of uneven stones in the Baptistry of St. Mark's in Venice, and with them all the feelings of joy and wonder that had accompanied his standing on them in that remarkable setting.

It was not simply the memory but the act of remembering, triggered by a present sensation—in this case, stepping on uneven stones—that brought Proust's protagonist such "delight". The spontaneous ability of the imagination to connect past with present, to know in the present a past experience with such clarity as to duplicate its emotional response, elicits for him a real sense of freedom. With memory and imagination at one's disposal, Proust seems to conclude, one need no longer be held captive by present emotional states. He argues on the basis of this experience that by means of memory and imagination, humans have the psychical ability to grasp the real and vital connection between how things *were* then, and how things *are* now. When exercised properly, this ability makes possible the "bliss" of transcendence. And is this not, I want to ask, an adequate description of Gadamer's "joy of recognition" in the *anamnesis* of aesthetic experience; as well as Newman's "feeling...of self-gratulation" prompted by the illative sense and its imaginative connections of past impressions with present experience?[406]

Though Proust and others of the romantic ilk think of the "joy" that attends such imaginative insights as expressed only in creative works of artistic "genius", there is no reason to suggest that imaginative flights into the sublime are confined to the talented few.[407] Imaginative powers are possessed by all, and may be

[406] In this connection, consider Joseph Addison's very Newmanian-sounding claim: "Our imagination loves to be filled by an object, or to grasp at anything that is too big for its capacity. We are flung into a pleasing astonishment at such unbounded views, and feel a delightful stillness and amazement in the soul at the apprehension of them...for a spacious horizon is an image of liberty, where the eye has room to expatiate at large on the immensity of its views". In Joesph Addison, *Collected Works*, III, ed. H Bohn (London: Bell and Sons, 1890), pp. 397-98.

[407] For the contrary doctrine, and a nice summary of the Romantic position, see Arthur Schopenhauer, "On Genius", in *The World as Will and Idea*, E Payne, trans. (New York: Dover Books, 1958), vol. 2, ch. XXXI.

disciplined and strengthened by anyone. Moments of illuminating *poesis* are to be found anywhere and at any time. "Poetically humans dwell on the earth", wrote the German poet Hölderlin [1770-1843], a phrase Heidegger was to take up as his ethical watchword.[408] Without some form of imaginative outlet, without the freedom and "ecstasy" of creative, intellect-driven thought, there can be no reconciliation with the felt-alienation and homelessness that so strongly characterises our present state of existence. The late novelist Italo Calvino writes to the point:

> The weight of living consists chiefly in constriction, in the dense net of public and private constrictions that enfolds us more and more closely...Perhaps only the liveliness and mobility of the intelligence escape this sentence...Whenever humanity seems condemned to heaviness, I think I should fly like Perseus into a different space. I don't mean escaping into dreams or into the irrational. I mean that I have to change my approach, look at the world from a different perspective, with a different logic and with fresh methods of cognition and verification.[409]

What is common to both human nature and artistic achievement, personal memory and public creativity, the "mobility" of intelligence and an escape from the world's "constrictions", is the willful claim to the human right to exercise one's mind imaginatively and freely; the right to hope for further space, even amidst the darkening of our present technocracy, for the "feeling of the sublime". Again, it is Wordsworth who speaks on our behalf, and this in the most evocative of terms:

> ...the soul
> Remembering how she felt, but what she felt

---

[408] Cf. Martin Heidegger, "Poetically Man Dwells", in *Poetry, Language, Thought*, A Hofstadter, trans. (New York: Harper & Row, 1971), ch. VII.
[409] Italo Calvino, "Lightness", in *Six Memos for the Next Millennium*, P Creagh, trans. (London: Jonathon Cape, 1992), p. 7.

> Remembering not, retains an obscure sense
> Of possible sublimity, to which,
> With growing faculties she doth aspire
> With faculties still growing, feelings till
> That whatsoever point they gain, they still
> Have something to pursue.[410]

However privileged we are to catch the occasional glimpse of a "possible sublimity", there is always something more beyond our reach; there is no end to human striving; insatiability and growth are written into the very fabric of Being. The "obscure" feeling the poet here describes, I want to suggest, is the same sort of tragi-poetic sense generated most acutely by the *religious* imagination. The religious imagination, as we have already seen, works through symbols to reach toward a knowledge, forever incomplete, of God. All vital knowledge of God, the kind that leaves us still with "something to pursue", is *symbolic*; which is to say representative; and ever in need, therefore, of imaginative interpretation before it can "speak" to our present situation.

Let me explain further. Consider Gadamer's doctrine of "anticipation" or "projection" where a fuller understanding is attained in the imaginative "from-to" transferral of meaning: it follows from this that where a *religious* understanding is expressed, meaning has been transferred *from* the personal experience of various religious symbols, and all else that arises from one's religious *Bildung, to* the being we call God. That such transferences are imaginative is implied by the fact that they clearly involve something more than logical deduction. According to the same Gestalt theory Gadamer uses in his description, imaginative projections are intuitive, and the process by which they are adduced inarticulate. This also was Newman's intent, we will recall, when he used the image of the mountain climber who "ascends how he knows not himself, by personal endowments...rather than by rule".

All of which leads me to conclude, after taking up my Newman-

---

[410] Wordsworth, *Prelude*, book II, 312.

Gadamer synthesis, that our knowledge of God as it arises from our engagement with religious symbols and experiences, is fundamentally an interpretative projection of self-understanding; which is itself given substance by *Bildung*, by a participation in the *sensus communis*, and by the kind of tacit reasoning—i.e. *phronesis*— engendered by other, not necessarily religious experiences. Or to put it more simply: our private, present sense of God is cognitively related to our imaginative sense of ourselves as this latter sense is given *religious* shape by the collective, public *memoranda* of religious traditions and beliefs. This model does not presume to say, as *per* Feuerbach and Freud, that a sense of God is *only* a sense of ourselves. To make that assertion would require going back behind religious traditions themselves to inquire as to where they come from; i.e. to inquire into the possibility of God's "self-revelation", and how it has come to be preserved in our religious traditions. This, however, is beyond my concern here.[411] What it *does* presume to say is that in the assertion of religious claims to a knowledge of God, wherever and whenever they are made, a great deal of human imagination is involved.

It also suggests that there are striking parallels between a poetic "feeling of the sublime" and a genuine interpretative experience of God arising from a symbolic encounter. *Poesis* and *mimesis* each engage the imagination and yield an expansion of horizon. Many people indeed, and not only poets and artists, have had the experience of feeling intensely the "huge significance of the present moment";[412] they "see" a sublimity in an otherwise ordinary thing or event, and from there the imagination takes over. Some describe these feelings as a "being at one with the universe"; some say they are the lineaments of God. In terms of my Newman-Gadamer synthesis, the difference between the two readings reflects a difference in how respective horizons of interpretation have been forestructured; i.e.

---

[411] On this question, see Keith Ward, *Religion and Revelation*, cited above.
[412] Michael Paffard, *The Unattended Moment* (London: SCM Press, 1976), p. 45.

how certain "first principles", *Bildung* and the *sensus communis* have been personally appropriated. In either case, each has the potential to function as real knowledge for the individual; as an epistemic centre around which the various facets of life are placed, giving to the whole a sense of order and significance. But this, of course, is no guarantee of their objectivity.

And so my synthesis to this point may sound a bit subversive. It may be thought a dangerous doctrine to assert that what knowledge we have of God we have in and through the imagination; that the religious imagination is no different in operation from the poetic imagination of the sublime; that in either instance it is a matter of projecting meaning from a subjective experience onto an imagined entity which, in objective terms, may or may not exist; and that whether one projects an ethereal feeling of universal connectedness, or one that senses the presence of the Christian God, it is merely a matter of personal taste. I might as well be saying that in matters of religion the imagination, here as elsewhere, concerns itself only with, in Sartre's words, "that which is not".[413] Perhaps this lengthy analysis of religious knowledge has led me to conclude, along with the American poet, Wallace Stevens, that "the final belief is to believe in a fiction, which you know to be a fiction, there being nothing else. The exquisite truth is to know that it is a fiction and that you believe it willingly".[414]

Were I to stop here, then the response to the above accusations would in each case be in the affirmative. To this point I have indeed been left with the Feuerbachian-Freudian assessment of religion as an unreal system of wish-fulfillments. For this, as we have seen, is exactly where Newman leaves us, *sans* church authority, and Gadamer, *sans* tradition. But this is not all that can be said, nor is it all that should be said. What I have been describing here is the role of the imagination in the formation of religious knowledge, and how

---

[413] Jean Paul Sartre, *The Psychology of the Imagination* (London: Methuen, 1972), p. 12.
[414] Wallace Stevens, *Opus Posthumous*, S F Morse, ed. (New York: Alfred Knopf, 1957), p. 163.

that knowledge differs little from other imaginative and interpretative forms of knowledge, especially the poetic. Yet what the imagination itself actually *is* has still to be discussed.

It has been said that as perception has to do with percepts, and conception with concepts, so imagination has to do with images.[415] I perceive a particular tree; I conceive of the concept of tree-ness; but I imagine a purple tree or a tree of solid gold as tall as the sky and as wide as a mountain growing on top of a church steeple or under the sea or on the moon, and so on *ad infinitum*. Note that my perception is bounded by a particular tree; my conception is bounded by the idea of tree-ness generated from all the particular instances of trees I have encountered; but my imagination is free, unbounded and as wild as my spirit allows it to be. It is no wonder that Aquinas would have nothing to do with it;[416] and that Plato long before him had banned the poets from his well-ordered republic.[417]

Clearly something more must be added. What if imagination's vibrancy and colour were given a sense of direction; were made to serve something outside itself, something higher and beyond its reach, yet able to assign its renderings both significance and purpose? A well-known passage from Augustine's *Confessions* shows us the way forward at this point. In the tenth chapter of book seven, Augustine describes his conversion from Manicheism to Christianity by way of Neoplatonism. This ideological change came about, he says, not by means of rational reflection and logic, but only as he "entered into [his] most inward self" and noted there *"supra mentem meam lucem incommutabilem"* ["an unchangeable light residing above my mind"]: *"supra"* not in a spatial sense, he goes on to explain,[418] but in the sense of a region of light and truth *other than* the familiar and the

---

[415] Cf. N D O'Donoghue, "The Mystical Imagination", in James Mackey, ed., *Religious Imagination*, p. 186.
[416] Thomas Aquinas, *Summa Theologica*, I. qu. I. a. 9, obj. i.
[417] Plato, *Republic*, book 10 *et passim*.
[418] Augustine, *Confessions*, VII, x. "Nor was it above my soul as oil is above water, nor yet as heaven above earth: but above to my soul, because It made me; and I below It, because I was made by It".

known; an ethical region of such dazzling brilliance and power that in its presence human horizons all but disappear. Augustine has described here, I suggest, something similar to the Kantian "sublime": both are trans-conceptual realms of inarticulate experience; both require the use of symbols to explain; both involve the imagination in their poetic renderings.

The passage ends, however, with a statement that seems to take the experience into another dimension altogether; a decidedly un-Kantian statement that comes quite unexpectedly in the context of an account concerning *intellectual* change by way of a light "above the mind". The statement is this: that "only *love* knows this light" [*caritas novit eam*], for the light itself *is* love:

> O Truth who art Eternity!
> And Love who art Truth!
> And Eternity who art Love!
> ...Thou didst beat back the weakness of my sight,
> Streaming forth Thy beams of light upon me,
> And I trembled with love and awe...[419]

In a later and more famous passage [X.17], this realm of light is invoked as "Beauty ever ancient and ever new". Here clearly we are in an imaginative world of Augustine's own creation, a world of human striving and struggle transformed poetically, imaginatively, into religious conviction. It is couched in a language of love by the call of Love. Impressed by the vibrancy of his own mystical experience, Augustine imaginatively translates two common conceptual realities—light and beauty—beyond their etymological borders into the "trembling" experience of a Presence, at once self-contained ["and Thou didst cry to me from afar, 'I Am that I Am'"] and conscripting ["I am the food of grown men; grow, and thou shalt feed upon Me"]. Through this poetically mediated experience of God, given substance by an active imagination, Augustine has entered into that state of

---

[419] Augustine, *Confessions*, VII, x. Cf. *City of God*, book XI, 28.

being I want to call "imaginative knowing".

There is a remarkable resemblance in style, vocabulary and content between this passage from Augustine and the well-known account Teresa of Avila gives of her vision of the "Holy Trinity".[420] Teresa tells us that, though her vision of the "three Persons" is an "intellectual vision" and "not imaginative", it nonetheless comes by way of the affective faculties:

> The spirit becomes inflamed by means of a cloud of surpassing brightness...In the extreme interior, in some place very deep within itself, the nature of which it does not know how to explain, because of a lack of learning, it perceives this divine company [i.e. the Trinity].[421]

Teresa's inward illumination is, as with Augustine's, both dramatic and definitive, establishing her in a new mode of being and acting. What binds them together is their shared experience of the beatific vision, following a period of introspective struggle and reflection, and preceeding the exercise of an active and creative imagination as it is allowed to speculate on what sort of image might best circumscribe the experience. In each case, the resulting vision (Augustine's flaming light of love; Teresa's cloud-enshrouded Trinity) is impressed *inwardly*: either upon the heart (Augustine) or soul-spirit (Teresa). In each case—and here lies the crux of the argument—the inward journey has been motivated by a profoundly felt need for clarity; for a new perspective from which to view the whole. The two descriptions stem from periods of real crisis (Augustine's vision from a feeling of existential angst, Teresa's from a series of debilitating illnesses), and yet they stand independent of their generative experiences, working their way into, and bringing greater illumination upon, the respective theological horizons of their

---

[420] Teresa of Avila, *The Interior Castle*, trans. Kieran Kavanaugh, OCD (New York: Paulist Press, 1979) in a chapter entitled, "The Seventh Dwelling Place", ch. 1. 6 (p. 175).
[421] Teresa of Avila, *The Interior Castle*, "Seventh Dwelling Place", I. 7.

locutors.

By implication we can conclude that it is human *eros*, the conscious, *felt* need for God—or more accurately, for some mode of transcendence that takes us beyond "the dense net of constrictions" in which our public lives trap us—that readies the recipient in heart and mind for the religious experience; and inspires the imagination to attain to new forms of religious description. All authentic religious expression flows from these *eros*-inspired moments whose depth, intensity and lasting value are in turn dependent upon the imaginative capacities of the one experiencing and describing them. It could be said, of course, that such description is merely an exegesis, a "leading out" of already existing states deep within the human soul; that religious experience and its articulation are merely forms of memorating certain aspects innate to the human condition that have long since been forgotten. This would fit well into the sort of Gadamerian version of *anamnesis* I detailed earlier; and is not far from Newman's understanding of ideological development in which spinning ideas suddenly click into place, releasing new insights. But for each, the argument is conditioned by an assumption that there is a real "other" there to evoke the memory, to cause the spinning to stop. So too the religious experience: it is an experience of something external to the self—a "non-human corrective presence", to use Brian Wicker's phrase[422]—that causes the self to withdraw into its own imaginative depths, to reflect upon its state in the world, and to search for fresh images by which to articulate that state *in relation to* the "other".[423]

One more point needs to be made. While both Augustine and Teresa share strikingly similar affective and intellectual experiences, the doctrinal explanation of each differs. For Augustine, the vision of

---

[422] Brian Wicker, *The Story-Shaped World* (London: Athlone Press, 1975), p. 12.

[423] The fundamental thesis of my work in *The Truth That We Are: Gadamer and the Ethics of Transformation* is that Gadamer's ethics requires the human self to define its present state always over against "the other", but that his system lacks a comprehensive enough "other" by which to accomplish this in any sort of ultimately satisfactory way.

light is articulated alternatively along the lines of Neoplatonic philosophy (where the metaphors of light and beauty are hypostasised) and a biblical existentialism—"I Am that I Am". Teresa's description, on the other hand, is coloured by her exposure to the dramatic climate of southern Spain, her friendship with the poet of the "dark night", John of the Cross, and her adherence to the Chalcedonian formulation of a Trinity-in-unity. If the two descriptions are intended to point to the same object, i.e. God, then clearly it is not the *explanation* but the *experience* underlying it that is the primary thing. Which is to say, theological mimesis is derivative, secondary, even parasitic upon something far more primordial. For behind every "ontic" formulation of the nature of God—as if God were a mere present-to-hand "thing", an "instrument" we may take up at will and enshroud in pragmatic terminology[424]—lies an ontological, pre-given openness of human being toward God that renders the experience of God possible in the first place. Thus prior to symbolic knowing, and more fundamental than imaginative knowing, there exists a third form which I want now, in closing, to describe.

EXPERIENTIAL KNOWING

Religious experience is that inward experience of an "other"— God, the sublime, the transcendent, etc.—whose nature is such that it inspires the imagination to use symbols—Light, Love, Beauty, Cloud of brightness, etc.—in its attempts at description. In doing so, these symbols are transformed from their ordinary, everyday system of referents to one that connotes *religious* meaning: wine becomes blood, a tree becomes a cross, Jesus becomes the Christ. This originative, religious experience of the "other" becomes itself, then,

---

[424] For the Heideggerian critique of the sort of "instrumental" and "present-to-hand" language used in modern technology, see Joanna Hodge, *Heidegger and Ethics*, ch. 2; and compare Gadamer, *RAS*, especially pp. 1-20.

another "other", inspiring its own series of visions, symbols and imaginative explanations, and so on. It is clear, therefore, that only by first understanding the religious "other-experience" can we hope to understand the kind of knowledge that stems from it.

There are, in my estimation, three main aspects of religious "other-experiences" that arise when, in Newmanian fashion, the subjectivity of the recipient is taken as a starting point: the emotional aspect, the givenness of the experience and its poetic expression. I want now briefly to take each of these in turn.

The religious "other-experience" is principally an experience of affection, or what we might call a heart-experience. It is a movement of the affective part of one's being that inspires the extroversion needed to reach out understandingly to the transcendent "other". One sees this movement powerfully expressed in the poems of John of the Cross. In his *On a Dark Night*, John writes:

> One dark night
> Fired with love's urgent longings
> —Ah the shere grace!—
> I went out unseen,
> My house being now all stilled
> ...With no other light or guide
> Than the one that burned in my heart.[425]

Here the soul goes out into the darkness of sensual deprivation in order to seek the Beloved because the heart has been priorly "enkindled" by the "flame of God's love".[426] Such an experience is described by John as "a certain longing for God"; and is interpreted as the feeling of being "attracted by the love of God". But this is tantamount to saying that imaginative elements are involved in his interpretation; otherwise the longing felt so deeply as a deprivational affect ("one dark night") would have remained unnamed. Because it

---

[425] John of the Cross, "On a Dark Night", in *Selected Writings*, trans. Kieran Kavanaugh, OCD (New York: Paulist Press, 1987) book one, preface (p. 162), stanzas 1 and 3.
[426] John of the Cross, "On a Dark Night", book one, ch. 11. 1 (p. 187).

is labelled as a longing for a divine Lover, it demonstrates the influence of pre-given "first principles" or "prejudices" appropriate to the *Bildung* of a Carmelite monk.   And yet, beneath these determinative forestructures of consciousness lies the more primordial, more existential affective "urgency" of John's *love* that inspired the search for theological delimitation in the first place. The light of God, after all, burns in his *heart*, not his *head*.

There are others who attest to the primacy of the heart with respect to religious experience. T S Eliot, well-read in the Christian mystics and ancient Buddhist teachings, in the final movement of his *Four Quartets* hints at the kind of religious awakening, the "midwinter spring", that comes to a heart frozen by despair:

> Midwinter spring is its own season
> Sempiternal though sodden toward sundown,
> Suspended in time, between pole and tropic.
> When the short day is brightest, with frost and fire,
> The brief sun flames the ice, on pond and ditches,
> In windless cold that is the heart's heat,
> Reflecting in a watery mirror
> A glare that is blindness in the early afternoon.
> And glow more intense than blaze of branch, or brazier,
> Stirs the dumb spirit: no wind, but pentecostal fire...[427]

Eliot speaks here of that experience when in the cold and dark mundanity of everyday life a revival of spirit occurs, stirring "the dumb spirit", suspending the normal passage of time "between pole and tropic".   Within Eliot's well-read horizon of understanding such openings are conceived of as religious experiences, initiated by a "pentecostal fire" and symbolised by "fire", "sun" and the feeling of "sempiternality". But note: their inspirational locus is the heart. In the same poem he speaks of "the drawing of this Love and the voice of this Calling" that inspires us "not [to] cease from exploration".[428]

---

[427] T S Eliot, *Little Gidding*, I.
[428] T S Eliot, *Little Gidding*, V.

And yet Eliot, in a manner not unlike Teresa's "cloud of surpassing brightness" and Augustine's *lucem incommutabilem*, speaks of "blindness".   Hence the exploration "Love" animates is "sempiternal", never ending: "And the end of all our exploring / Will be to arrive where we started / And know the place for the first time".

Each metaphor Eliot uses evokes the sense of an unlimited horizon; of a spiritual journey without maps; of a spirituality ever *en route*. Were one to extend Eliot's poetic sensibilities into a theology, one would be forced to say that religious description is profoundly untrue to the nature of the experiences that underlie it whenever it claims perfection or completion.   Sometimes determinative consciousness leads to excesses—the Crusades, the Inquisition, sectarianism—hence, the need always to be wary of the fixity and narrowness of dogmatism. For if the originative "otherness" of God is the source of religious experiences, the *fontes* of all truth viewed *sub specie aeternitatis*, it is ever welling-up in new and creative ways; for the vehicle of its up-rising, i.e. human existence, is itself *ever on the way*.

Secondly, religious experiences are generally experienced as something *given*. John of the Cross qualifies his inspired longing for God in an aside that reflects its true source: "Ah the sheer *grace*"! Eliot's imagery—the "watery mirror" that reflects "a glare that is blindness"—seems to allude to the Pauline experience of being suddenly, unexpectedly blinded by "a bright light from heaven".[429] The "givenness" of the experience implicit in these claims indicates that states of religious awareness bring with them the feeling of "passivity" or lack of control. At their most intense, the recipient of such experiences feels overwhelmed by a presence greater than himself; a will that forces one's own into temporary abeyance.[430] As Baron von Hügel writes,

---

[429] Acts: 9:3.
[430] This is the fourth of William James' four principle characteristics of mystical experience in his *Varieties of Religious Experience*. Cf. Michael Cox, *A Handbook of Christian Mysticism* (London: The Aquarian Press, 1986), p. 26.

the further the soul advances [in the religious life], the more it
sees and realises the profound truth that all it does and is, is
somehow *given to it*..., all the soul's actions tend to coalesce
to simply being, and this being...comes more and more to be
felt and considered as the simple effect of the one direct action
of God alone".[431]

The turn from active productivity to passive receptivity is central
to the tradition of prayer that Teresa inspired, and is carefully
described in the fourth mansion of her *Interior Castle*. In the first
three mansions the disciple seeks God actively as a gardener might
draw water from a well to irrigate his plants; in the fourth mansion,
however, rains falling from heaven water the garden apart from any
human help. John of the Cross as well describes the givenness of
religious experience with a wide range of images, the most powerful
and well-known of which is that of a bride swept away by the
bridegroom's love. So absorbed by the bridegroom is the bride that
she loses sight of herself: "I no longer tend the herd / Nor have I any
other work / Now that my every act is love".[432]

Religious experiences seem often to come unbidden, are
unexpected, at times unwanted. This does not exclude personal
activity altogether, of course. Sometimes religious experiences are
prompted by the kinds of "off-balance" mental states that result from
serious illness (Teresa: tuberculosis), innocent suffering (John of the
Cross: imprisoned for "heresy"), extreme fear or anxiety (Augustine:
guilt over past sins). At other times experiences are induced by
deliberate exercises of concentration, ascetic disciplines, sensory
deprivation, and at a more extreme end, drug use. But even in these
instances, the descriptions that follow almost always testify to an
outside reality "breaking-in", and in light of which all preparations
are made to seem futile. Like John of the Cross' "wound of love" that
was inflicted while the disciple quietly slept on the Beloved's breast,[433]

---

[431] Baron von Hügel, *The Mystical Element in Religion* (London: Hodder and Stoughton, 1923),
vol. 1, p. 369. Italics added.
[432] John of the Cross, "Spiritual Canticle", in *Selected Writings*, p. 225.

experiences of God initiate in some way with God, even if coloured both before and after the fact by a healthy dose of *gebildete* imagination.

Thirdly, there is a continuity of expression between religious experiences and those fostered by a poetic imagination. John's *Dark Night* and Wordsworth's *Intimations of Immortality* are of a piece precisely because they are imaginative renderings of profound experiences that defy the ability to express them straightforwardly. Such experiences are unique, highly personal and unrepeatable. Yet in each case the "other-experience" is the same: a moment of illumination strikes the recipient—St. John's "fire burning in the heart" or Wordsworth's "fountain light"—releasing poignant intimations, "thoughts which lie too deep for tears" or insights into "the life of things".[434]   Essentially, both religious and poetic experiences are experiences of an expanding "depth" in perception; of openings into worlds even *beyond* the perceptual:

> And I have felt
> A presence that disturbs me with the joy
> Of elevated thoughts; a sense sublime
> Of something far more deeply interfused,
> ...and in the mind of man:
> A motion and a spirit, that impels
> All thinking things, all objects of all thought,
> And rolls through all things.[435]

The mystic thus labours under the same fundamental burden as the poet: both must contend with the utter inadequacy of human language to convey sublime experiences to others, along with the "urgent" desire so to convey those experiences. Thus we witness the common use made by religious writers and poets of symbols and metaphors. The experiences that underlie their descriptions are no

[433] John of the Cross, "The Ascent of Mount Carmel", stanza 8, in *Selected Writings*, p. 268.
[434] Cf. O'Donoghue, "The Mystical Imagination", p. 195.
[435] From Wordsworth, *Lines Composed a Few Miles Above Tintern Abbey*.

less real for their ineffability. For the recipient, the *reality* of what he apprehends is, at least for him, beyond all doubt. "All the utterances of the mystics", writes David Knowles, "are entirely inadequate as representations of the mystical experience, but they bring absolute certainty to the mind of the recipient".[436] Nevertheless, the *attempt* to express what is by nature inexpressible is nearly always made. For at the heart of all genuine religious experience is the passion to communicate.

These then are three aspects of the religious "other-experience": it is primarily and centrally a heart-experience; it is for the most part a gift, sought after but not achievable or even knowable outside of a giver-receiver relationship; and it is best expressed in, and has continuity with, poetic form. We are still left with the primary question, in what sense are "other-experiences" a source of real knowledge? Do Teresa's visions or John of the Cross' poems give rise to true understandings of the nature of God, and God's relationship to humans?

Briefly and in light of the above, I would want to answer this by arguing that given the nature of the human experience of the sublime, of religious and poetic "other-experiences", there is the *possibility* of real, epistemic if not ontological contact with God, the realm of supra-intellectual Light; and that, considering the large amount of well-documented evidence testifying to the experiential reality of this possibility, one could reasonably push this in the direction of a *probability*. The question as to whether a *particular* witness to a probable sublime realm is to be accepted or rejected is a question of the nature of the evidence presented, and of the trustworthiness of the individual involved. If we follow Richard Swinburne's famed "principle of credulity", that we should believe normally truthful and reliable people until they are discredited,[437] then we would have to conclude that, for the most part, the *onus probandi* rests upon the

---

[436] Cited in Cox, *Handbook of Christian Mysticism*, p. 25.
[437] Richard Swinburne, *The Existence of God* (Oxford: Oxford, University Press, 1979), pp. 25ff.

prosecution.

Still, we are without any consistently helpful epistemology of religious knowing if we fail to move beyond mere credulity. If religious knowing is principally metered by affective experience, by the *Bildung*-mediated imagination, then religious epistemology must look carefully at the question of the personal subject, and of the subjective experience of God. When it has done so, it ought to have found, as indeed both Newman and Gadamer had found, that there exists a tension between the originative "other-experience" and those imaginative conceptualisations that always follow. This tension resolves itself only by moving toward more and more language, toward greater and more complex forms of communication, toward theological development, mimetic expansion, *fusion*. This is only natural, and though far from the ideal (a perfection of non-verbal, intuited communication), in *this* life it is only to be expected.[438]

There is also a movement in the opposite direction, however. Even for the one who is *gebildet*, who has been educated from without by means of "personal influence" and the *sensus communis*, and from within by a "tactful" receptivity to conscience, a genuine experience of what he or she has been conceptualising and imagining and speaking about for a long time comes only after the fact. Or, at a more extreme end, it may be the case that, no matter how skilful one is in theological construction, one may over time become aware that the reality of which one speaks has never really been understood at all; nor ever can be understood.

Gadamer illustrates this with his principles of "application" and "performance" when they reject a universal notion of conceptual

---

[438] Cf. Karl Rahner, *Foundations*, p. 16. Rahner posits the tension between "reality" or "original unity" and its "objectifying concepts" to be inherent to human existence, and is only transcended in and through an increasing amount of language. This particular problem George Steiner calls the "dominance of the secondary and the parasitic". And it is in part a product of an errant understanding of the discipline of hermeneutics. Rather than the now common notion of hermeneutics as a science of translation, of the communication of meaning from one language system into another, it is perhaps best seen, Steiner suggests, as an "acting out" of meaning so as to give it "intelligible life". Cf. George Steiner, *Real Presences* (London: Faber and Faber, 1989), pp. 7-8.

reality in favour of making reality a matter of personal *experience*.
Every real experience, says Gadamer, is an event of "undeception" in
which we are made aware of those of our vain imaginings that do not
"fit" reality.[439] For Gadamer, in his own words, this is "ultimately a
religious insight", for each such experience of true reality is ultimately
the "experience of the borders of human finitude, beyond which
stands the divine".[440] The truly experienced theologian, therefore, is
one who knows the limits of speech; who expects that, over time, the
human experience of God will lead to the disassembling of even the
most fondly-held of constructs; that replacing out-worn and cliché-
like metaphors with fresh, experience-ladened names for God is at
the heart of his or her task.

The stress on experience is also central to Newman's
understanding of the notion of religious knowledge. It is the marriage
of abstract ideas and concrete action that Newman terms "real
apprehension". So faith is said to "be a venture, to involve a risk";[441]
for ultimately, religious knowledge rests upon the coöperation of
intuition and imagination, rather than ratiocination alone.[442] The
grist for faith's mill is that "sacred impression", derived from past
experiences and that, lying "prior to" propositions of faith, "acts as a
regulating principle...ever present upon the reasoning".[443] Religious
knowledge, then, is "not a mere letter" but an "august token of the
most simple, ineffable, adorable facts, embraced, enshrined, according
to its measure, in the believing mind".[444]

This focus on a subject-oriented epistemology of religious
knowledge is, as I have tried to show throughout this study, a deeply
Newmanian concern. And inasmuch as it is so, it shows considerable
parallels with Gadamer's aesthetic and hermeneutical philosophies.

---

[439] Gadamer, *TM*, p. 319.
[440] Gadamer, *TM*, p. 320.
[441] Newman, *US*, p. 217.
[442] Cf. Andrew Louth, *Discerning the Mystery*, p. 138.
[443] Newman, *US*, pp. 335-36.
[444] Newman, *US*, p. 336.

Together these two important thinkers point toward a method of theological progress in which the concept or image of God, and the symbols that point to God, are creatively, imaginatively, with less self-deception and more self-understanding, thought through and articulated in terms of the experience, demands and needs of each new situation in which believers find themselves. At the heart of this method is the two-fold aim of developing the idea of God through new concepts and images, while at the same time translating the relevance of traditional notions into an ever wider circle of human experience.

This will, of course, force theological discourse to concentrate its efforts upon what is happening within the individual and his or her imaginative processes of reasoning. It is here that theology merges its efforts with, among others, psychology, physiology and the philosophies of art, history and language. Clearly this is to invite a great deal of tenuousness into what we call our knowledge of God. Yet it seems that we are left with no other way of going about an epistemological survey of religious knowledge without running the risk of de-humanizing it altogether.

BIBLIOGRAPHY

Newman's works:

AVS   *Apologia Pro Vita Sua*. London: Sheed and Ward, 1976.

Arians   *Arians of the Fourth Century*. London: Longmans, 1833.

DD   *Essay on the Development of Doctrine*. 1878 version. Notre Dame, Indiana: Notre Dame Press, 1989.

ECH   *Essays Critical and Historical*, two volumes. London: Longmans, 1891.

US   *Fifteen Sermons Preached Before the University of Oxford*. London: Longmans, 1845.

GA   *Grammar of Assent*. London: Notre Dame Press, 1979.

HS   *Historical Sketches*, three volumes. London: Longmans, 1906.

Idea   *The Idea of a University*. Chicago: Loyola University Press, 1927.

LD   *Letters and Diaries*. London: Longmans, 1908.

PN   *Philosophical Notebooks*, two volumes. E Sillem, ed. Louvain: Nauwelaerts Publishing House, 1969.

PPS   *Plain and Parochial Sermons*, eight volumes. London: Longmans, 1891.

STA   *Select Treatises of St. Athanasius*, J H Newman, trans. London: Longmans, 1843.

Newman-related works:

Butler, Joseph. *Analogy of Religion, Natural and Revealed*. Oxford: Clarendon Press, 1874.

Brown, David, ed. *Newman: A Man for Our Time*. London: SPCK,

1990.

Chadwick, Owen. *From Bousset to Newman*. Cambridge: Cambridge University Press, 1987.

Coulson, John. *Religious Imagination*. Oxford: Clarendon Press, 1981.

_____. *Newman and the Common Tradition*. Oxford: Clarendon Press, 1970.

Cross, Frank L. "Newman and the Development of Doctrine", in Church Quarterly Review, January (1933) 245-57.

Hick, John. *Faith and Knowledge*. Ithica: Cornell University Press, 1957.

Jaki, Stanley, ed. *Newman Today*. San Francisco: Ignatius Press, 1989.

Jost, Walter. *Rhetoric Thought in John Henry Newman*. Columbia, South Carolina: University of South Carolina Press, 1989.

Ker, Ian. *John Henry Newman*. Oxford: Oxford University Press, 1988.

_____ and Hill, Alan, eds. *Newman After a Hundred Years*. Oxford: Clarendon Press, 1990.

Lash, Nicholas. *Change in Focus*. London: Sheed and Ward, 1976.

_____. *Easter in Ordinary*. London: SCM Press, 1988.

_____. *Newman on Development*. London: Sheed and Ward, 1975.

_____. *Theology on Dover Beach*. London: Darton, Longman and Todd, 1976.

_____. *Theology on the Way to Emmaus*. London: SCM Press, 1986.

Newman, Jay. *The Mental Philosophy of John Henry Newman*. Dallas: Waterloo Press, 1986.

Nichols, Aidan, OP. *From Newman to Congar*. Edinburgh: T & T Clark, 1990.

Reardon, B.M.G. *From Coleridge to Gore*. London: Longman's Group, Ltd., 1971.

Walgrave, Jan. *Newman the Theologian*. London: Hodder and Stoughton, 1960.

_____. *Unfolding Revelation: The Nature of Doctrinal Development*. London: Hutchinson, 1972.
Weatherby, Harold. *The Keen Delight*. Athens: University of Georgia Press, 1975.

Gadamer's Works:

PA   *Philosophical Apprenticeships*. R. Sullivan, trans. Cambridge: MIT Press, 1985.
PH   *Philosophical Hermeneutics*. D. Linge, trans. Berkeley: University of California Press, 1976.
RAS   *Reason in the Age of Science*. Cambridge: MIT Press, 1981.
RB   *Relevance of the Beautiful*. R. Walker, trans. Cambridge: Cambridge University Press, 1986.
TM   *Truth and Method*. Second edition. London: Sheed and Ward, 1975.

Gadamer-related works:

Foster, Matthew. *Gadamer and Practical Philosophy*. Atlanta: Scholars Press, 1991.
Hirsch, E.D. *Validity in Interpretation*. New Haven: Yale University Press, 1967.
MacIntyre, Alasdair. "Contexts of Interpretation: Reflections on Hans-Georg Gadamer's *Truth and Method*", <u>Boston University Journal</u>, 24(1) 1976, 41-46.
Heidegger, Martin. *Basic Writings*. D. F. Krell, ed. London: Routledge, 1977.
_____. *Being and Time*. J. Macquarrie and E. Robinson, transls. New York: Harper and Row, 1976.
_____. *Early Greek Thinking*. San Francisco: Harper and Row,

1975.

_____. *Poetry, Language, Thought*. A. Hofstadter, trans. San Francisco: Harper and Row, 1971.

Silverman, Hugh, ed. *Gadamer and Hermeneutics*. London: Routledge, 1991.

Thiselton, Antony. *The Two Horizons*. Grand Rapids: Eerdmans Press, 1980.

_____. *New Horizons in Hermeneutics*. London: HarperCollins, 1992.

Warnke, Georgia. *Gadamer: Hermeneutics, Tradition and Reason*. Stanford: Stanford University Press, 1987.

Weinsheimer, Joel. *Gadamer's Hermeneutics: A Reading of Truth and Method*. New Haven: Yale University Press, 1985.

General Works:

Bowker, John. *The Sense of God*. Oxford: Clarendon Press, 1973.

Bullough, Edwin. *Aesthetics: Lectures and Essays*. London: Bowers and Bowers, 1957.

Bungay, Stephen. *Beauty and Truth*. Oxford: Clarendon Press, 1989.

Calvino, Italo. *Six Memos for the Millennium*. London: Jonathon Cape, 1992.

Caputo, John. *Radical Hermeneutics*. Bloomington: Indiana University Press, 1987.

Carr, Thomas K. "Let Being Be". *Times Literary Supplement*, 16 February (1996): 13.

Cohen, Ted and Guyer, Paul, eds. *Essay's in Kant's Aesthetics*. Chicago: Chicago University Press, 1982.

Collingwood, R.G. *The Idea of History*. New York: Oxford University Press, 1956.

Cox, Michael. *A Handbook of Christian Mysticism*. London: The

Aquarian Press, 1986

Crouther, Paul. *The Kantian Sublime*. Oxford: Clarendon Press, 1989.

Danto, Arthur. *Analytical Philosophy of History*. Cambridge: Cambridge University Press, 1968.

Dillistone, F.W. *The Power of Symbols in Religion and Culture*. New York: Crossroad, 1986.

Emerson, Ralph Waldo. *Essays*. London: Everyman's Library, 1906.

Gallagher, Shaun. *Hermeneutics and Education*. Albany: State University of New York, 1992.

Geertz, Clifford. *The Interpretation of Cultures*. New York: Basic Books, 1973.

_____. *Anthropological Approaches to the Study of Religion*, M. Banton, ed. London: Methuen, 1968.

Giddens, Anthony. *New Rules of Sociological Method* London: Basic Books, 1976.

Hodge, Joanna. *Heidegger and Ethics*. London: Routledge, 1995.

von Hügel, Baron. *The Mystical Element in Religion*. London: Hodder and Stoughton, 1923

John of the Cross. *Selected Writings*. Kieran Kavanaugh, OCD, trans. New York: Paulist Press, 1987

Kaelin, E F. *Heidegger's Being and Time*. Tallahassee: University of Florida Press, 1987.

Kaufman, Gordon. *Theological Imagination: Constructing the Concept of God*. Philadelphia: Westminster Press, 1981.

_____. *In Face of Mystery*. Cambridge: Harvard University Press, 1993.

Kuhn, Thomas. *The Structure of Scientific Revolutions*. Chicago: Chicago University Press, 1967.

Lindbeck, George. *The Nature of Doctrine*. Philadelphia: Westminster Press, 1984.

Loder, James. *The Transforming Moment*. Colorado Springs: Helmers and Howard, 1989.

Louth, Andrew. *Discerning the Mystery*. Oxford: Clarendon Press,

1983.

Mackey, James, ed. *Religious Imagination*. Edinburgh: University Press, 1986.

Macquarrie, John. *Jesus Christ in Modern Thought*. London: SCM Press, 1990.

Nietzsche, Friedrich. *The Portable Nietzsche*. W Kaufmann, trans. London: Penguin, 1982.

_____. *Ecce Homo*. W Kaufmann, trans. New York: Vintage Books, 1967.

Pafford, Michael. *The Unattended Moment*. London: SCM Press, 1976.

Polanyi, Michael. *Personal Knowledge*. Chicago: University of Chicago Press, 1958.

_____. Marjorie Green, ed. *Knowing and Being*. Chicago: University of Chicago Press, 1969.

Popper, Karl. *Objective Knowledge*. Oxford: Oxford University Press, 1972.

Price, H.H. *Belief*. London: Bearge Allen and Unwin, 1969.

Prosch, Harry. *Michael Polanyi: a Critical Exposition*. Albany: SUNY Press, 1986.

Rahner, Karl. *Foundations of Christian Faith*. New York: Seabury Press, 1978.

Rilke, Rainer Maria Rilke. *Selected Letters (1902-1926)*. R Hull, trans. London: Quartet Books, 1988.

_____. *Selected Poetry*. S Mitchell, ed. and trans. New York: Vintage Books, 1982.

Scott, Nathan. *Towards a Poetics of Belief*. Chapel Hill: University of North Carolina Press, 1985.

Swinburne, Richard. *The Existence of God*. Oxford: Oxford University Press, 1979.

Taylor, Charles. "Interpretation and the Sciences of Man", *Review of Metaphysics*, 25 (1971): pp. 3-51

Teresa of Avila. *The Interior Castle*. Kieran Kavanaugh, OCD, trans. New York: Paulist Press, 1979

Verene, Donald. *Vico's Science of Imagination*. Ithica: Cornell University Press, 1981.

Wach, Joachim. *Types of Religious Experience*. Chicago: University of Chicago Press, 1957.

Ward, Keith. *Religion and Revelation*. Oxford: Oxford University Press, 1994.

Wicker, Brian *The Story-Shaped World*. London: Athlone Press, 1975.

Winch, Peter. *The Idea of a Social Science and its Relation to Philosophy*. 3rd ed. London: Routledge and Kegan Paul, 1964.

Wright, T.R. *Theology and Literature*. Oxford: Basil Blackwell, 1988.

THOMAS K CARR, formerly Junior Dean of Oriel College, Oxford and Tutor in Philosophy and Religion at Oxford University, is presently Assistant Professor of Philosophy and Religion at Mount Union College in Alliance, Ohio. He earned his BA from Willamette University, his MDiv from Princeton Theological Seminary, and his MPhil and DPhil degrees from Oxford University.